Be a
Better
Boss!

Robert S. Walsh, MBA

Walsh, Robert S.
        Be a Better Boss

p.cm.

ISBN – 10: 1492704431
ISBN – 13: 978-1492704430

1. Business & Economics / Management   2. Leadership
10 9 8 7 6 5 4 3 2 1

boss (noun)

leader, manager, supervisor, decision maker, head honcho, big kahuna, the one the buck stops with.

Contents

"Good judgment comes from experience,
and a lot of that comes from bad judgment."

— Will Rogers

Chapter One

Three Bricks in Your Foundation

If I were to ask you to describe your leadership philosophy, what would you say? Would you have an answer? Have you considered the question?

Certain core paradigms are essential to sound leadership, and among them, these three in particular:

1. Leadership is influence.

2. To be influential, leaders must have awareness.

3. A leader's focus should be outward; toward their team. They should do what is right for their team above themselves.

As the first three bricks necessary when building the foundation of an effective leader, these are essential. Leaders who have them operate with increased wisdom, while leaders who lack them have trouble; and sometimes a lot of trouble.

I wish I could tell you that I learned about these foundational concepts by reading them in a book, or listening to the sage wisdom of an experienced leader.

In truth, I learned them the hard way, and I'd like to tell you about it by sharing a story from my past. Quite frankly, it's a story that is embarrassing, but I feel it's worth sharing for reasons I'll tell you about afterward.

It happened many years ago, somewhere below the surface of the Pacific Ocean...

> *I was a Chief Petty Officer in the U.S. Navy serving as a Nuclear Propulsion Plant Supervisor onboard the fast attack submarine, U.S.S. Parche (SSN-683). I had twenty-three nuclear trained personnel working for me.*
>
> *These men were literally the cream of the crop. Navy "nukes" are among the smartest and most capable people in the Navy.*
>
> *Down the hall, or passageway, from the crew's mess, or enlisted dining facility, was the "Leader-board" that had about two dozen brass nameplates mounted on it. Each was engraved with the name of one of the management staff that currently held leadership positions onboard the ship. Some of these nameplates were shiny and new, some were older and tarnished, and all were in their proper place... except mine.*
>
> *One fateful day, mine went missing.*
>
> *I realized it was gone when I went to the head (restroom) back in the engine room. I looked down, and there, glued to the back wall of the urinal, was my nameplate!*

I lost it! Everyone who worked for me probably had a truly delightful time urinating on my nameplate and laughing their butts off!

We have a saying in the Submarine Force for times like these:

**When in trouble, or in doubt,
run in circles, scream and shout.**

This was wisdom lost on the forlorn nameplate owner.

I threw open the door and grabbed the first poor soul I could find and "supervised" as he removed the nameplate and gave it to me - after he'd sanitized it, of course.

I went off into a corner, nameplate in hand, to stew. Alone now, the reality of it all hit me in the chest – full force.

Oh my God! My guys hated working for me! Worse, to do this, they must actually hate me as a person!

This was feedback of the worst kind and it gnawed at my heart; raw and extremely hurtful feedback.

How in the hell did this happen to me? I was devastated. I was a rotten leader. They knew it and I knew it too.

However, this event was to become a pivotal moment in my life as a leader. Howard Swain, Chief-of-the-Boat (aka: "COB"), one of the best leaders who ever walked the decks of a submarine, was there to help, teach, and guide me.

Howard always seemed to know everything that went on. Later that day, he walked up, put his hand on my shoulder and said, "Bob, I heard about the nameplate, and I'm going to tell you the truth... You don't know what the hell you're doing!"

How true; Howard never pulled a punch.

He went on to say, "When you're ready, which needs to be right now by the way, we'll talk and help you fix this problem."

Howard became my mentor.

I didn't know it at the time, but over the course of the next eighteen months, Howard would teach me to be a good leader like no one else could have.

He was always there with his patient ear and easy-going style to help, guide, coach, and most importantly – to model excellence in leadership. Chiefly he'd ask questions and help me figure out the angles as each small challenge or situation arose.

Sometimes he'd give me the right words to say, or just stand back and tell me to figure it out for myself.

Over time, I came to understand how I got in these shoes. I knew I had been a good leader until the day I was advanced to Chief Petty Officer, when I made a fatal error, actually a series of them to be accurate.

To start with, I tried to be the same guy I was before I put that uniform on. I was an easy going, very friendly leader of a different group, on another ship. They were peers and subordinates, and they were also my buddies. I wanted things to be the same now that I was a Chief, but I didn't understand that my new team wouldn't see me in the same way because I was a Chief.

So, I was either coming across as their buddy and pal, or when that failed – another great mistake – I got very coercive with predictable results.

My people distanced themselves from me because they didn't know who was going to show up that day. Maybe it would be nice Chief Walsh who just wanted to be one of the guys, and acted that way. Or maybe it would be nasty Chief Walsh who jammed things down their throats. I happily distanced myself from them as well, and all of this behavior got me in trouble.

I became almost completely ignorant of what was going on with my team. I had no clue about what was happening in their lives outside of work, or on the job. It became commonplace for me to show up and be the last to know what was going on, when I was expected to be a real Chief and be the pivotal person.

As time went on, things degraded further and I hated being there.

I'm sure you could see it in my eyes; I certainly could when I looked in the mirror or in the eyes of those I led. I had little or no confidence. I could frequently feel a certain hollowness in my chest. I had trouble sleeping and relations with my family became strained. I hated going to work and actually tried to hide during the day.

Vacations, holidays, and sick days became brief moments of "relief."

However, all this changed with Howard as my mentor.

Over the next year and a half, my confidence grew and Howard's presence shifted from mentor to colleague. What a great feeling it was to have the confidence that comes from knowing you're doing a good job as a leader. There is no substitute.

I owe a great deal to Howard Swain's guidance and patience. Thank you Howard!

There are many things I hope you learn from that story. Chief among them is the hope that it sparks your thinking about what you need to change in your own life as a leader.

My reasons for sharing it also include:

1. Being open and honest; to practice what I'll be preaching.

2. To illustrate that no matter how low you might go, it can be fixed. Never give up!

3. To emphasize the importance of having a true friend and mentor to help you stand up, fight, and change.

And last, but not least:

4. When you fix real issues that brought you out of a deep and dark place, you'll never repeat them again... right?

Wrong. Unfortunately #4 isn't true; at least not for me.

It seems that we are all doomed to forget what we've learned and repeat our mistakes over and over. That way we get to improve ourselves again and again, right?

Really, I'm talking about our human flaws to illustrate that being open and honest means being realistic about how things work. So no sugar-coating on anything as we look at being a better boss.

A Look in the Mirror

That brings me to a question I have for you:

What are the three most important things you need to change about yourself to be a more effective leader?

Some things to consider might be:

1. What worries you and keeps you up at night?

2. What situations do you shy away from?

3. What have others told you that you need to work on?

Please take out a piece of paper and list everything that comes to mind; then choose the top three things you need to change. Hang onto these so you can work with them later.

Key Points of Chapter One

1. Leadership is influence.

2. To be influential leaders, we must have accurate awareness.

3. A leader's focus should be outward; toward their team. They should do what is right for their team above themselves.

4. Genuine leaders operate outside their comfort zones, being faithful to the team and putting them first.

5. Never give up. Instead find a good mentor and work to fix what you need to fix.

6. A true friend and mentor will help you stand up, fight, and change.

Chapter Two

Leadership Bushido

Let's revisit the question we started the last chapter with. If I were to ask you to describe your leadership philosophy, what would you say? Would you have an answer? Have you considered the question?

Howard – you remember Howard – told me something once that made me think about it. He said, *"Bob, if you have no idea who you are or what you're all about, then your team won't be able to count on you and will have no confidence in you."*

Well obviously, I needed to know who I was and what I stood for. I needed a philosophy; a code; a foundation to operate from.

Why? Because there is a process and it works like this:

- Your code forms your paradigm, your foundation;
- Your paradigm defines how you think and feel;
- How you think and feel determines how you act;
- How you act results in how others think and react to you;

- How others think and react to you will determine your effectiveness as a leader.

Therefore, I had to consciously choose the code I was going to lead by, and that I and my team would live by.

It was easier not to have a code; I lived without one for years. Just make it up as you go along and lead by the seat of your pants. But to have no code is still a choice and my choice resulted in being blown about by the winds of expediency, emotion, and chance.

This was certainly not the leader my team wanted or deserved. I was not a genuine leader in the eyes of my people. This was very clear at those key moments when my team expected me to make a clear decision, and they got... something much less.

While searching with the intent of developing my code, I came across the code of the ancient Japanese Samurai, called Bushido, which contained Seven Virtues:

GI (integrity)

REI (respect)

YU (courage)

MEIYO (honor)

JIN (compassion)

MAKATO (honesty)

CHU (loyalty)

Today, we might call these virtues our "Core Values."

These seemed like a good place to start. I could certainly look up to a leader who lived by these seven. So they became seven bricks in building my foundation; my leadership bushido.

A Code is Not a Set of Rules

This reminds me of another little story I'd like to share with you.

Once upon a time....

> *It was a dark night and my wife, Denise, and I were driving home after visiting with friends for the evening. We were the only ones on the road.*
>
> *When we came up to a stop sign I slowed down to what I thought was a safe speed and didn't quite stop. After all, there was not another car in sight.*
>
> *As we started up again, Denise looked over at me with a wry grin and said, "You know, rules and laws like speed limits and stop signs are really nothing more than suggestions to you."*
>
> *"Yes, I guess that may be true," I replied, laughing.*
>
> *"That's really the way you see all rules, isn't it?" she chortled back.*
>
> *"How do you see it?" I asked, grinning.*
>
> *"Rules are made for a reason, and I follow the rules," she asserted.*

Without thinking very much, I replied, "Well, I guess it comes from my independent nature, but the way I see it, there are times you should follow the rules and times when it's OK to use your own discretion."

"I see," she said. "So that's what you're going to tell the police officer when you get stopped?" She is such a smart-ass. I had to laugh again.

"Well, I, ummmm..." (I had no comeback!)

"Yeah, I thought so. I just don't know about you Walsh! You are so bad!" she said while shaking her head and rolling her eyes.

This ended out little talk about rules.

Later on, while I was thinking about what Denise and I had quipped, I recalled what a very wise former mentor had taught me...

It was just another routine day - assigning work, monitoring results, dealing with problems; the mundane stuff of leading my team.

I had just finished dealing with a procedural issue with Jesse, one of my subordinates, when my mentor came by and pulled me aside. He asked me what I had just done, in a rather odd way, saying something like, "I heard what you just agreed to with Jesse. I know everyone around here thinks that is the right way, but you do know that's not what the policy says, don't you?"

"Um, no, actually I thought that was what it says and

frankly, we've always done it that way."

"Famous last words; we've always done it that way," he replied. "It's time for some calibration. I have three or four things I've learned the hard way for you to think about."

He laid them out for me.

"First, as a leader, you need to know the book like the back of your hand because the day will come when you have to violate it and you'd better be able to do so intelligently."

"Second, at all other times, you need to set the example and follow the rules, policies, and procedures. Your team expects this and deserves this from their leader."

"Third, if the book needs to be changed then change it, but follow the book in the meantime; or get or give permission to violate it in writing, until it can be changed."

And last, *"Your people need to be able to depend on where you stand on things. Violating the rules as a matter of routine undermines their confidence in your leadership – even if only in small ways – but believe me, they take note of this and not in a good way; it undermines the team."*

Over the years, his lessons have stuck with me as part of my Leadership Bushido.

I still treat some rules as suggestions, like the stop sign, but I do so with full awareness of the consequences and impact it may have on others.

After all, a code is not a set of rules; it's a set of guiding principles.

This can be subtle stuff – but this is what the best leaders I know do every day. It's the right thing to do for the team, which makes it the right thing for us as leaders.

That brings us to my second question for you:

What is your leadership bushido?

If you don't have your code formalized and written down, now is the time to do that. If you do have yours written down, then now is a good time to review and revise it.

As an example, my Leadership Bushido (as it exists today) is on the following two pages. Please feel free to draw from it as you develop, review, and revise your own.

My Leadership Bushido

1. **Influence** – Remember that leadership is influence. Be aware of the impact of your words and actions.

2. **Awareness** – Be perceptive; have situational awareness; gain an accurate, factual picture. Use this as the basis for your decisions and actions; minimize reactionary, emotional decisions.

3. **Focus on others**– Place the needs of your team and others you are serving above your own needs and wants. Do what is right for them instead of what you personally prefer. Challenge your zones of comfort and discomfort.

4. **Honesty** – Strive to always be honest. Without honesty, there is no trust.

5. **Integrity** – Do what you say.

6. **Respect** - Show respect to all others in what you say and do.

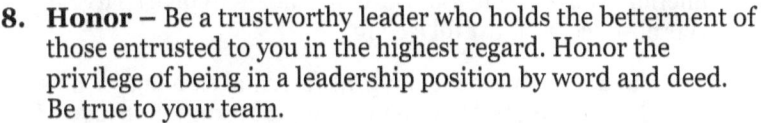

7. **Courage** – Do what you fear in order to do what is right. Stand for fairness and justice.

8. **Honor** – Be a trustworthy leader who holds the betterment of those entrusted to you in the highest regard. Honor the privilege of being in a leadership position by word and deed. Be true to your team.

9. **Compassion** – Try to put yourself in the shoes of others by asking them what those shoes are all about. Treat others with compassion and empathy.

10. **Loyalty** – Honor your commitment to the people, ideas, and things you have pledged to be loyal to.

11. **Knowledge** – Seek out and learn the things you should know. The day may come when you have to improvise, and your knowledge will help you do so intelligently with wisdom.

12. **Initiative** – Take care of things as soon as possible, without excuses or procrastination. Both on the positive and negative; take action.

13. **Self-control** – Exercise self-control over your emotions, selfishness, and other negatives. Seek help when you falter; pray for God's help; self-control is one of the fruits of the Spirit (Gal 5:22).

14. **Set the example** – Set the example in all things. Follow the rules, be on time, do excellent work, be well groomed and dress well, behave well.

15. **Communications** – Speak in an exemplary manner. Don't criticize, condemn, or complain. Communicate with clarity, Listen well with the intent to understand, not the intent to respond.

16. **Be strategic** – Always have a clearly defined vision, mission, and goals; communicate them regularly. Delegate, never micro-manage. Think and act strategically; let the team take care of production. Lead people, manage things.

17. **Be positive and approachable** – Enough said.

18. **Work your way out of a job** – Develop the entire team to function well without you. Develop leaders to take charge in your absence, not just fill a chair.

19. **Innovate** – Always be looking, asking, and striving for new ways that are better. Don't fight change. Never fall in love with a certain way, or your own way; be ready to change as necessary.

20. **Be thankful** – Being a leader is a privilege. Always be thankful for what the team does. Show your appreciation in abundance.

21. **Lighten up and smile** – Don't take things too seriously, find the humor. Make the burdens of others seem lighter and more enjoyable. Spread good feelings by smiling... often!

My leadership bushido has evolved a great deal over time. I've always felt free to add or subtract from it as I saw fit; as it made sense.

One personal decision I made is to limit the list to twenty-one items. I did this because:

1. It's easy to have too many items, with small items gumming up the proper functioning of the bushido. Such items can usually be rolled into bigger, more generalized or important items.

2. Twenty-one is a nice number!

Before you read on, please spend an appropriate amount of time working on your own leadership bushido. Maybe even sleep on it.

I mention this as there have been many who've lost sleep while setting up a formal leadership bushido. Not a bad thing to lose sleep over, I think, but...

> *One lady I was working with told me she'd been unable to sleep an entire night, but happily had gotten her bushido done.*
>
> *I asked her to tell me what she'd come up with.*
>
> *Her bushido was about two-dozen items long, and when she was finished telling me about them, she looked at me for my feedback.*
>
> *So I told her, "You've got a solid list there, good job, but you're missing one really important item."*
>
> *She glanced at her list, and puzzled she asked, "What's missing?"*
>
> *"Get a good night's sleep, every night!" I said with a smile.*

Key Points of Chapter Two

1. If you have no idea who you are or what you're all about, then your team won't be able to count on you and will have no confidence in you.

1. A code is not a set of rules; it's a set of guiding principles.

2. Twenty-one is a nice number!

To download a free PDF that includes the 21 items in my leadership bushido, go to the "Free for you" section of the "Products" page at www.BeaBetterBoss.com and click on "Your Leadership Bushido."

Chapter Three

Leadership and Management Effectiveness Self-Evaluation

Now that you've started on your leadership bushido, it's a good time to more formally reflect about yourself as a leader and manager. This self-evaluation concentrates on ten areas of leadership competency:

Communication - Feedback - Emotions - Teamwork
Delegation - Judgment and Decision Making
Self-Management - Organization and Planning
Leadership & Influence - Honesty and Integrity[1]

Each competency area is described by five statements for you to evaluate using the following scale:

4 = Excellent; 3 = Very Good; 2 = Marginally Good;
1 = Needs Significant Improvement

Thinking about these may also help you further clarify your leadership bushido. Remember, no one else will see how you rated yourself, or read your comments; this is for your eyes only.

---

[1] Adapted from the "Leadership & Management Effectiveness Profile" © Be a Better Boss, LLC

1: Communication

_____ I communicate clearly, both orally and in writing.

_____ I am an effective listener; focused, fully present, and attentive.

_____ My non-verbal's such as facial expressions and gestures match what I'm saying.

_____ I listen with the intent to understand rather than respond; I don't cut people off, finish sentences for others, or dominate the conversation.

_____ I take responsibility for making sure communications are effective.

4 = Excellent; 3 = Very Good; 2 = Marginally Good;
1 = Needs Significant Improvement

Please record your reactions below. Include whether this is an area of comfort or discomfort for you, and anything you know you need to work on.

2: Feedback

_____ I am open and honest in offering feedback to others about job performance.

_____ I give praise effectively and in direct proportion to excellence of job performance.

_____ I ensure criticism is constructive rather than destructive or punitive in nature.

_____ I do not shy away from offering constructive feedback to avoid confrontation.

_____ I seek out and thoughtfully consider feedback received about my own performance.

4 = Excellent; 3 = Very Good; 2 = Marginally Good;
1 = Needs Significant Improvement

Please record your reactions below. Include whether this is an area of comfort or discomfort for you, and anything you know you need to work on.

3: Emotions

_____ I do not take things personally or blame others.

_____ I am even-tempered.

_____ I am personable, likeable, and approachable.

_____ I show emotions but also exercise appropriate self-control; I do not express negative personal views in public when inappropriate.

_____ I do not take things too seriously or too frivolously; I show appropriate concern.

4 = Excellent; 3 = Very Good; 2 = Marginally Good;
1 = Needs Significant Improvement

Please record your reactions below. Include whether this is an area of comfort or discomfort for you, and anything you know you need to work on.

4: Teamwork

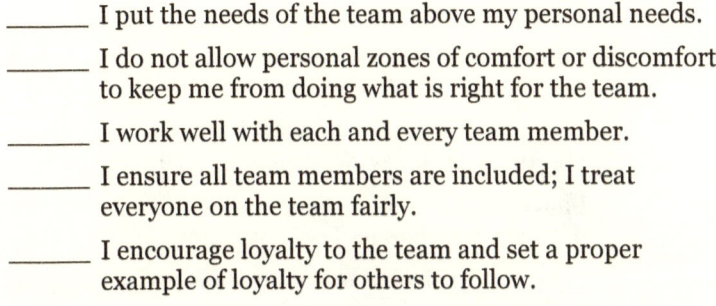

_____ I put the needs of the team above my personal needs.

_____ I do not allow personal zones of comfort or discomfort to keep me from doing what is right for the team.

_____ I work well with each and every team member.

_____ I ensure all team members are included; I treat everyone on the team fairly.

_____ I encourage loyalty to the team and set a proper example of loyalty for others to follow.

4 = Excellent; 3 = Very Good; 2 = Marginally Good;
1 = Needs Significant Improvement

Please record your reactions below. Include whether this is an area of comfort or discomfort for you, and anything you know you need to work on.

5: Delegation

_____ I delegate the work fairly.

_____ I utilize delegation as a development tool to increase the capabilities of team members.

_____ I do not undermine what is delegated by taking over, micromanaging, or violating the "chain of command."

_____ I have sufficient technical / professional knowledge of the work being done; I stay proficient.

_____ I stay aware of what team members are working on and the status of their work.

4 = Excellent; 3 = Very Good; 2 = Marginally Good;
1 = Needs Significant Improvement

Please record your reactions below. Include whether this is an area of comfort or discomfort for you, and anything you know you need to work on.

6: Judgment and Decision Making

_____ I seek and utilize input from others when making decisions.

_____ I take the time to make well thought out decisions; I am not prone to impulse.

_____ I make sure decisions are clearly defined and well communicated.

_____ I think about the impact of my actions; how others think and feel.

_____ When mistaken, I take responsibility and work to correct mistakes.

4 = Excellent; 3 = Very Good; 2 = Marginally Good;
1 = Needs Significant Improvement

Please record your reactions below. Include whether this is an area of comfort or discomfort for you, and anything you know you need to work on.

7: Self-Management

_____ I set the example by being on time, well organized, dressing properly, and being properly self-controlled.

_____ I'm a self-starter; I don't procrastinate.

_____ I'm well organized with paperwork, correspondence, time management, deadlines, etc.

_____ I personally follow the rules, policies, and procedures.

_____ I know my own weaknesses and work to correct them.

4 = Excellent; 3 = Very Good; 2 = Marginally Good;
1 = Needs Significant Improvement

Please record your reactions below. Include whether this is an area of comfort or discomfort for you, and anything you know you need to work on.

8: Organization and Planning

_____ I set a clear vision and clear plans of action; I communicate these with clarity.

_____ I ensure that rules and processes enhance the ability of the team to function.

_____ I always have a clear plan and ensure it is up to date as things change.

_____ When tasked with hap-hazard planning from higher-ups, I work to ensure the team makes these plans workable.

_____ I do not destructively criticize the plans and decisions of others in public; I work to support and help improve the organization and higher-ups.

4 = Excellent; 3 = Very Good; 2 = Marginally Good;
1 = Needs Significant Improvement

Please record your reactions below. Include whether this is an area of comfort or discomfort for you, and anything you know you need to work on.

9: Leadership and Influence

_____ I am an effective leader within the team, with higher-ups, and when interfacing with other teams.

_____ I am an assertive and influential leader; I stand up for the team.

_____ I adapt how I lead and manage to fit the situation; I'm not stuck in my ways that feel comfortable to me.

_____ I am appropriately involved; not a micro-manager or under-involved.

_____ I am both a good leader and a good manager in proper balance.

4 = Excellent; 3 = Very Good; 2 = Marginally Good;
1 = Needs Significant Improvement

Please record your reactions below. Include whether this is an area of comfort or discomfort for you, and anything you know you need to work on.

10: Honesty and Integrity

_____ I walk my talk; what I say is what I do.

_____ I can be counted on to tell the truth.

_____ I am trustworthy; a person of high character and ethics.

_____ I take responsibility to lead. I do not say things like, "I can't do anything about that."

_____ I set an example of leading and managing that others look up to and want to follow.

4 = Excellent; 3 = Very Good; 2 = Marginally Good;
1 = Needs Significant Improvement

Please record your reactions below. Include whether this is an area of comfort or discomfort for you, and anything you know you need to work on.

Competency Ratings Summary

To calculate your scores, total up your answers for a particular area, plug that total into the table below, and then divide by the factor shown (.20). The results will be on a 100% scale.

Example:

Teamwork	17 ÷ .20 =	85 %

1. Communication _____ ÷ .20 = _____%

2. Feedback _____ ÷ .20 = _____%

3. Emotions _____ ÷ .20 = _____%

4. Teamwork _____ ÷ .20 = _____%

5. Delegation _____ ÷ .20 = _____%

6. Judgment and
   Decision Making _____ ÷ .20 = _____%

7. Self-Management _____ ÷ .20 = _____%

8. Organization & Planning _____ ÷ .20 = _____%

9. Leadership & Influence _____ ÷ .20 = _____%

10. Honesty & Integrity _____ ÷ .20 = _____%

Consider setting improvement goals if:

1. The grade for an area on this summary page is lower than 85%;
2. Looking back at individual items, if you rated yourself a 2 or 1;
3. For items you noted as areas of discomfort or that you know you need to work on, regardless of the grade.

"It is necessary for us to learn from others' mistakes. You will not live long enough to make them all yourself."

- Admiral Hyman G. Rickover

Chapter Four

Things to Ponder and Fine Points

In the Chapter 3 you did a formal self-evaluation of specific leadership and management competencies.

This chapter contains writings on a variety of topics; things for you to self-reflect about in a less formal manner.

As you think about these, please record your reactions. Be aware of areas of discomfort, and things you know you need to work on.

All of your efforts will come together as goals and action plans when we get to Chapter 11. Please go there and take a look if you need a framework for clarity at this point.

Listening

When I was young, ambitious and motivated, I remember having what I thought was a "brilliant" idea about how to do something better. I don't remember what the idea was, but I do remember that when I tried to share my great insight with my supervisor, I was cut off in the middle of a sentence and told that my idea wouldn't work. "We've done that before," or "We've tried that before and it didn't work," I don't remember the exact words my supervisor used, but the message was clear.

However, I do remember feeling hurt and frustrated because I wasn't listened to. I remember walking away saying something like, "Why didn't he listen to me? He didn't even let me get my point across. What's wrong with him?" I left that encounter a little less motivated, and a little gun-shy toward suggesting anything in the future.

Has that ever happened to you as a subordinate? Have you ever failed to listen to another, as a leader?

Listening is a discipline that many leaders do not practice effectively. I would go so far as to say that, in my experience, listening is the most ill practiced leadership skill, yet we all know that we need to listen effectively to lead effectively.

Patient listening

My mother used to tell me that, "Patience is a virtue." Maybe your mother said the same thing to you. Why would my mother consider patience to be a virtue? Possibly because so many people fail to exercise patience – and they frequently show it in their poor listening skills!

Patient listening doesn't just automatically happen. It requires conscious thought.

The truth is that we all have to exercise our conscious intent to be patient because listening and patience are active, not automatic actions. We can't condition or train ourselves to do these two properly without consciously thinking about them as we do them.

> **"The deep knowing that is wisdom arises through the simple act of giving someone or something your full attention."** - Eckhart Tolle

Honor others by "being there"

There are two ways in which we typically listen – with patience or with the intent to respond.

Patient listening is a hallmark of genuine leaders. Conversely, listening with the intent to respond is a negative habit born of impatience. It typically shows itself by either our interrupting the other person when they are speaking, or by not fully listening and so misunderstanding what the other person says.

The next time someone is communicating to you, give that other person the honor of your full attention. Listen intently with the goal of hearing and really understanding what that person is saying – not half-listening or listening with the intent of responding (getting your two-cents in).

Stay aware and minimize allowing your mind to drift. Effective listening honors those who are speaking to you. Be known as a leader who patiently listens and understands. You'll have a better team and you'll make better decisions, because wisdom is a product of knowing.

Patient listening is a virtue!

Five factors missing from text or email

When we text or email, we are relying on words alone - so exactly what are we missing when we lack all physical presence? There are at least five vital items:

1. The look in each-other's eyes;
2. Facial expressions;
3. Hand movements and body language;
4. The context of the room and surroundings - sights, sounds, smells;
5. The intangible "aura" of the other person; their presence.

Think back about specific times in the past when communications broke down and went wrong for you. Was one or more of the five factors missing or the culprit?

Cement this knowledge in future action by calling or meeting when you know you should.

Any personality type can be a good leader

When I conduct team training or 1-on-1 coaching for the Myers-Briggs Type Indicator® (MBTI®), I frequently get asked, "What's the best personality type for a leader to have?"

The answer: Any personality type can be a good leader.

Some may think that you need to have some sort of big command presence and low booming voice to lead. But consider the quieter, reflective leader who speaks in few words. Like Margaret Thatcher, or Gibbs from NCIS.

Since any type can be a good leader, there are situations where a particular type may have some advantage, but just as sure as the sun will rise, their type will be a hindrance in other situations.

So whatever type you may be, you can be a good leader. It's about developing methods that work for you in order to effectively use the skills required to influence others.

Leading your team through change

Many people tend to choose the concrete and predictable over the abstract and unseen; Comfort over Creativity. That may be one reason people resist change, and maybe why some fear new and creative pathways.

Think about this when you ask your team for new ideas and creative visions. Then be prepared to give them your empathy, patience, and understanding.

Allow time for things to sink in; again, be patient.

The net result is likely to be better, more creative ideas and easier acceptance to the changes they may bring.

On the other hand, resisting change is actually in your mind to some extent - specifically in the neural pathways you have formed.

No one likes to change, not even the best leader, because the ways we have learned to think (our neural pathways) feel comfortable to us. Even if we hate them, we feel a sense of comfort in our own ways because of this.

Allow yourself and others this; resistance to change is natural for everyone. The only way to achieve change is to feel discomfort as we re-program our neural pathways.

No pain, no gain - it isn't just physical!

Seek out feedback

Feedback is the breakfast of champions, be a more genuine leader by seeking it out.

Maybe buy a cup of coffee for a trusted senior member of your team and simply ask them, "How am I doing as a boss?" You may just be amazed at what you find out.

Thirteen common mistakes that leaders make

There are many things we do as leaders and managers that we could improve upon if we thought about it in the moment. Here are thirteen common mistakes that make life as a leader more difficult, along with some suggestions on how we might do things better.

Think about how you do business as you read these over, and think about how some small changes in these areas could help you be a better and happier boss!

1: Not accepting personal responsibility and accountability

As leaders we are always accountable for the actions and outcomes of the people on our team. But sometimes we may find ourselves saying things like, "It's not my fault, Bill made the mistake," or, "I did a great job" instead of "My team did a great job."

To avoid these mistakes, don't blame a team member when speaking to your boss or others outside the team – take responsibility as the leader when things go wrong, then hold the responsible team members accountable to you to fix the problem.

Likewise, give credit to the team when things go right and be humble in the background.

2: Micro-managing

Do you feel like you have to make every decision? Can team members make certain decisions then inform you as the leader?

If you went away for an hour, would the team still function? Would decisions still be made? Do you find yourself having to take time out of meetings to check up on the team?

Failing to empower people can result in a weak team, or a "Non-Team." Tap into the talent of team members and develop them so that the team will function without you.

This frees up your time as the boss and allows you to lead creatively; with foresight rather than having to be tied up as a "Micro-Manager." Your people are looking for you to do just that: formulate strategies, solve problems, and make decisions.

To avoid this mistake, change or strengthen your attitude that acknowledges the notion that sharing power multiplies the effectiveness of a team. Give your people the power and cut the managerial apron strings. You can always take the power back if it becomes necessary in a crisis, but then remember to back off and give the power back to the team when the crisis subsides.

3: Focusing on outcomes instead of shaping attitudes

Focusing on outcomes is like treating a symptom instead of the disease. Bosses who do this usually find themselves chasing their tails – never quite solving why things keep going wrong.

Instead, realize that work performance improves in direct proportion to healthy attitudes and mental discipline. Remember that:

$$\text{Thoughts} \;\rightarrow\; \text{Words} \;\rightarrow\; \text{Actions} \;\rightarrow\;$$
$$\text{Habits} \;\rightarrow\; \text{Character} \;\rightarrow\; \text{Destiny}$$

Superior team performance is the destiny of the wise leader who takes the time to form his or her team with the above formula.

Get to know your team members and value their strengths. Live by a simple rule; think in terms of how the other person thinks and consciously work to influence them to be a strong team member.

When people feel valued and feel that the leader cares about them, they'll return that caring with an attitude of gratitude.

4: Joining the wrong crowd

The water-cooler gossip.
The practical joker.
The negative office politics crowd.
The sit on the sidelines troublemaker.
The talk behind your boss's back crowd.
The talk behind your team member's back crowd.
The "Sky is falling" over-react to everything crowd.
The upper level management criticizer.
The idea criticizer.
The YOU fill in the blank—criticizer.

To avoid this, don't join what you know is a wrong crowd. In every case, someone will lose respect or trust for you. Once someone loses respect or trust for you, it will be a hard thing to regain, if it ever can be.

5: Leading everyone the same way

Short and sweet, people are different. If you try to lead and manage every person the same way, those that don't fit your style will not respond the way you want them to.

If you use the wrong style, you'll be doing things like yelling when you should be listening, setting goals when you should be setting the pace, or asking what others think when all they really want is for you to make a decision. You're the one who'll lose the most in the end because you're the one doing the wrong thing.

To avoid this mistake, get to know each person that works for you and experiment with the correct mix of communication and motivational tools to find out what works for each one. Little things like asking an experienced worker's opinion, or giving someone a chance to learn a new job they think is exciting. With a little experience, you'll be easily able to "crack the code" on each person and lead each one the right way.

6: Failing to ask for advice

There is a priceless amount of help available to the leader who has the maturity to ask for help when needed. The secret is, no matter how senior or experienced the boss; we all need advice from time to time to help us. For example, we may need to ask for ideas to solve problems we've never seen before or to strategize something we want to say to someone, or to get another opinion on a plan or schedule we've written.

When you first started out as a leader, you probably asked a lot of questions. As we mature, we must be sure not to lose this valuable source of wisdom. To avoid this mistake, establish and maintain a solid network of workers and managers alike, which can be your trusted mentors and advisors.

7: Exercising management by exception

Management by exception means that we manage by concentrating on what's going wrong.

The problem is, if we go looking for problems, we will find them, even the ones that don't matter. In some cases, we may even create problems by approaching life with a pre-conceived notion of negativity. Worse, we may get a huge feeling of accomplishment for having solved so many things.

The key to avoiding this mistake is to concentrate on the positive, while still being aware of problems. People shy away from negativity and are drawn to the positive and optimistic. If you want to lead effectively, you must be able to see and communicate the positives. Besides, the important problems will probably find you all by themselves.

8: Letting friendships affect your decision-making

There is nothing basically wrong with the boss being someone's friend, except that you cannot allow your friendships to affect your decision-making. If done wrong, others will probably see you as granting preferential treatment and being unfair.

Also, it is likely that someday you'll have to make a hard decision "against" your friend, or need to discipline your friend. They may feel betrayed and may say, "How could you do that, I thought you were my friend!"

The way to avoid this mistake is to leave your friendships at the door in all matters of professional performance and grant no extra privileges to anyone based on anything other than what is fair. Do not confuse this with being friendly, which is just fine. Remember, it's all in the eye of the beholder, and as the leader, you are showing your people how you should be thought of by your actions.

9: Failing to set, monitor, and enforce standards

Standards and rules are set in one way or the other, but there will be standards.

When a manager sets a standard and then allows it to be violated or worse yet, violates it him or herself, then a new standard has just been set.

Or, if the leader complains about a standard that has been set by another manager, that is the same as violating it in the minds of the team. Either way, what the leader says or does will be justification for everyone else to "Follow the Leader" and violate the standard.

"Do as I say, not as I do," has never been and will never be an acceptable way to lead. The team will almost always label the manager that tries this as being a hypocrite. There is no faster or surer way to destroy a team.

To avoid this mistake, it is important that you set proper standards (or support other managers' standards) and make sure they are supported and adhered to by everyone, especially you. Following the rules will just be normal if you do it this way and very few rules or standards will cause anyone to have a problem.

10. Not providing adequate training

When a new person comes on the job, or an experienced person starts a new job, the biggest disservice suffered can be a lack of adequate training. In this, we're talking about on the job training where you might be tempted to just assign the new person to whoever is currently doing the job. But is this the right person to train others?

Training another is frequently an entirely different matter than being good at doing the job and it requires a different set of skills. Also, some people who really know a job may willfully withhold knowledge with the notion that they gain increased job security from being the only one who "knows."

Another training issue that frequently crops up is that we might assume a certain level of knowledge because an employee comes to us from another company. Still another issue, especially in large companies, is the notion that the training department will do all the training for you.

To avoid this mistake, get involved in the details of how knowledge transfer and training are being accomplished and become active in making sure it is effective.

11. Not effectively addressing sub-standard performance

It happens so easily. An employee does a job inadequately and you choose to look the other way... you say nothing. You might do this because you are a little intimidated by an experienced employee. Maybe you hope that the problem will just go away. Maybe you have another reason.

Whatever the reason, we must fight that tendency and refuse to condone sub-standard job performance. Do this by providing good usable feedback, not punishment.

In private, talk to the person about his or her behavior with the intent of changing that behavior. Make sure to stick with the person's behavior and the standard that is not being met. If it gets emotional and he or she starts to take it like criticism, go back to their behavior vs. the standard and tell them your goal is to help them meet that standard and fulfill their responsibility to the team. If appropriate, formal documentation should be done also.

12. Not using informal recognition to motivate

We all need to be told we've done a good job and the best leaders dole out informal rewards regularly; it strengthens the team.

This has double the impact when you can do it in front of others, especially strangers.

Example: When you take a VIP on a tour and introduce him to Sue by saying, "Mr. Jones, I'd like you to meet one of the most knowledgeable punch press operators in the plant," the impact is obvious.

13. Trying to influence through manipulation

The two major tools of manipulation are fear and rewards. Both of these usually prove to be counter-productive in the end; they result in short spurts of activity and do nothing to build the team. Both get people to produce for the wrong reasons.

Historically, fear has probably been the most widely used "motivator" and the message used is usually something like, "produce or suffer." This is not to say that some behaviors should not be confronted, but this should done properly using constructive feedback and in private.

Equally ineffective is using a carrot on a stick type reward. Take away or fail to produce the promised reward, and performance goes down.

Over time, both manipulative rewards and fear will, if used as illustrated here, produce less of an effect as people become immune to them.

Perfection isn't required

A supervisor of mine once told me that, "Perfection isn't required, excellent is good enough!" While he was joking, there are some leaders who do expect perfection. They forget themselves.

We are all human, and we make mistakes.

If leaders expect too much, they may create a working climate that inhibits all the great things humans bring to work, like creativity and trying new things that involve some risk.

Allow others their humanity. Be there with them when they fail, not over them. They will appreciate it, and you'll be happier too - both with them and with yourself!

Honor those who work for you

On certain days like Labor Day, or Administrative Professional's Day, we are asked to remember those who work for us. Better yet, resolve to remember the excellence of the people who work for you every day!

Here are three tangible ways to honor those who work for you:

1. Be a leader who puts the needs of the team first, above your own.

2. Give praise to team members for all they do, not just the special things that stand out. Remember the grunt work!

3. Treat everyone on your team with high honor and respect, as you would your CEO.

Your attitude in leading others

Keep your promises and deliver more than you said you would.

This is a great customer service adage, but maybe more important for the attitude you should take with your team.

Be kind to others when they fail

We all know that learning from our failures is one key to success. But for leaders there is an added dimension - How do we treat others who work for us when they fail?

Be a better boss by forgiving and being kind to others when they fail. It's easy to feed another person's self-criticism at a moment of failure when they feel low. But a mature leader recognizes these moments as opportunities when they can help bolster another's self-esteem. It is a true act of genuine leadership.

Pessimism is addictive

Enthusiasm is addictive; so is pessimism.

As leaders, we are in a unique position to influence others, especially those who work for us, in one of these directions or the other.

Be a better boss in two ways: First, influence others with intent and in a positive way by being enthusiastic and encouraging others. Have a "can do" attitude.

Second, help those who express pessimism to shed their gloom-and-doom and turn a corner by being genuine, open, honest, and again, enthusiastic and encouraging. You can do it!

Praise your boss too

Everyone needs to know they are appreciated – even your boss.

Lead up by praising your boss. Find something you genuinely appreciate about the person you work for.

Then find the right time, praise them for this, and shake their hand.

If you're self-employed or you're the top leader, give praise to someone else who hasn't heard it enough.

Feedback model

1. Giving Feedback (constructive criticism)

    a. Before giving feedback:

        i. If you are uncomfortable or fear confrontation, discuss this with your mentor prior to offering feedback.

        ii. Practice (role-play) what you're going to say with your mentor and let him or her coach you through handling likely negative responses.

        iii. Remember it's not you against them; it's them vs. their responsibility to the team. It's not them doing what you say; it's the higher purpose of them doing what's right for the team.

    b. While giving feedback

        i. Start by asking for the other person's self-assessment. If they reply with the same thing you were going to talk about, you're done. If they say it; they get it.

        ii. If needed, give feedback;

            1. Face-to-face is best;
            2. Be honest, frank, kind, and understanding;
            3. Be specific, focus on behavior;
            4. Give constructive suggestions;
            5. Avoid overloading;
            6. Invite response, listen properly.

2. Receiving Feedback

    a. Listen properly and thank the other person.

    b. Take ownership, but don't take it so personally that you get emotional.

    c. Let them know when it's difficult to hear;
        i. If it's untrue, disregard it;
        ii. If it's unfair, stay calm;
        iii. If it's justified, learn from it.

    d. Set goals and turn up your behavior.

    e. Ask for more... there's always more.

An easy, yet somehow rare way of praising

Look around your workspace, and you may notice that people tend to keep thank-you notes they receive. They may even have them posted for all to see.

Make this part of praising others more effective by thanking team members in a hand written note from time to time. Use good quality thank you cards that show you took time – not a yellow sticky.

A personal note of thanks has impact because it has become a rare way of communication.

Negative emotions get in the way

Someone once said that leadership is 90% mental, and the other 10% is... mental.

When we are logical and our thoughts are well ordered - and we stay on top of them - we can all be highly effective leaders.

One thing that gets in the way are negative emotions; fear, anger, taking things personally, and several others. These can take us down the wrong - unthinking - path as leaders.

Be a better boss and think out an action plan to better control your negative emotions. It is a challenge you can achieve. Hang tough boss!

Maintain a good work / life balance

Every day, remember those who are important in your personal life. Don't let your professional life cause you to do things, or fail to do things, you will regret later. It's really not worth it.

Especially during the various holidays throughout the year, when you are off, place your loved ones first above any work that may have to be done because you are in charge.

Celebrate and be thankful for one-another.

The three C's

Everyone wants to destructively criticize, condemn others, and complain at times. We call these the "3-C's." When the boss does one or more of the 3-C's, the result is usually an obvious and unnecessary burden on the team.

Be aware of what you say and how you say it; avoid the 3-C's.

If you really do need to vent, do so in private with your own boss, mentor, or trusted peer – but not with the team.

Use everyday non-verbal's to make a good impression

Whenever I meet a person who gives me one of those awkward, soft, wimpy handshakes, it leaves a strong negative impression. The last time it happened, it was the first thing I talked about later on with my friend.

Evoke good emotional responses in others by remembering the importance of these three significant non-verbal's:

1. Male or female, have a solid, firm handshake;
2. Look people in the eye;
3. Have appropriate facial expressions.

The non-verbal impressions you leave behind can either enhance or degrade your ability to lead. These are some of the more subtle skills of effective leadership - make sure they work for you!

Calm and sure works best

Good leaders are effective at two things that require a great deal of introspection and humility; Dealing with bumps in the road, and making changes.

Be a better boss by tuning out the negative voices in your head when you or your folks hit those bumps in the road.

As in golf – the last shot, the one that went bad, doesn't exist.

When things go wrong, let your emotions die down, then deal with the situation at hand in a straightforward, logical way.

Calm and sure works best for everyone.

Know your people

Are there people on your team that you really don't know very well? Or perhaps it's just been hard to find the time to interact?

Take the time to personally visit the people on your team that you haven't interacted with very much. Chat with them about how things are going, their families, the news, but try to minimize talking about work. Make sure you end with a handshake and a smile.

Set the tone of your team

The tone of your household depends on how family members treat each-other. Fathers and mothers alike, tend to set that tone.

And so it is with the team you are on at work, where your leadership tends to set the tone.

Don't be tone deaf!

Think about the tone of your team. Not to be too corny, but is the team singing in harmony? If not, you as the leader need to act.

Remember, your team is a reflection of your leadership - maybe more than you'd like to admit. So work to set a great tone and a great team!

Email and texts can undermine delegation

Are e-mail & text messages hurting your team? In the old days before smart devices, when the leader was away, they usually left someone else in charge and delegated their authority.

But today, increased access has degraded delegation as a primary tool to develop new leaders.

Be a better boss and leave someone else in charge while you're away. Then, ensure you don't undermine them by running the show via e-mail or text.

Reserve electronic access to you for the one who should have it - the one you left in charge!

What, not how

George S. Patton once said, "Don't tell people how to do things, tell them what to do and let them surprise you with the results."

Be a better boss by <u>not</u> telling others how. Instead, ask them to tell you about their ways and methods – after they are all done!

Increased trust, creativity, and self-confidence are just three benefits that team members might reap from you holding back a little.

Multi-tasking overload?

How many things do you think you can do properly at the same time?

Well, if one is a learned repetitive activity, like driving a car and the second requires a high degree of concentration, like texting... the negatives are obvious. Yet many leaders think that multi-tasking is a good thing and over-do it.

Be a better boss by putting more thought into the multi-tasking your team members are trying to perform.

What we sometimes ask of others is a far cry from walking and chewing gum at the same time!

You can't fake knowing

You can't fake knowing something, and in this case we're talking about events and goings-on.

As leaders we must seek out the details of what's happening and be good at asking questions. We must also be strong-willed enough to keep on asking questions until we understand the answers.

It must also be the norm for others to keep you informed. If someone on your team knows something that you should know, it is their responsibility to tell you. Even if it's bad news; especially if it's bad news!

Hiding the truth is not okay because that means that you'll be finding out the hard way. You may even end up making poor or catastrophic decisions because you didn't know any better.

You must be known as a leader that makes it okay for people to tell you the truth. There cannot be a penalty for being truthful; otherwise people will not be open and honest with you. This includes you over-reacting and "shooting the messenger."

Strategic vision for your team

Good leaders are people of strategic vision.

Be a better boss by thinking about each individual on your team and what your highest vision for each of them is.

Develop a plan for how you can help each person achieve the vision you have for them. Discuss this with them.

When it's wrong to manage

How should you handle a team member who has a small performance issue? Let's say it's something relatively minor yet annoying; like repeatedly failing to keep their online calendar up to date.

It is all too common to deal with these kinds of issues by trying to manage them. Such things as the manager keeping very tight tabs on the issue (micromanagement), sending them to training, or taking on part of the responsibility by agreeing to send them daily reminders.

None of these will solve the problem because this is not a time for managing the issue. It's a time for effective leadership; coaching, mentoring, and performance counseling.

Keep the responsibility where it belongs, with the other person, and lead them to doing things the right way by doing what good leaders do best; influence them!

Honesty and integrity above all else

Think about the best leader you've ever personally known. Consider for a moment, what were the key traits that made that person such a great leader?

Some things that might come to your mind are initiative, common

sense, fairness, experience, even-handedness, goal orientation, a self-starter, integrity, honesty, or a good listener.
Now, consider the following scenario...

> *You are a line supervisor working for a company that manufactures high quality stainless steel fasteners for the aerospace industry.*
>
> *It's three o'clock in the morning and Bill, one of your senior Quality Assurance inspectors, is tired because he was out partying with friends instead of sleeping before his midnight shift. He "nods off" for a few key seconds and misses an automated Quality Assurance rejection alert on a batch of fasteners. He discovers the error and "fixes" his mistake by doing a manual verification inspection and "updating" the written records – removing all evidence of the occurrence.*

If you were the boss, what would you expect of Bill – the person who made this error? Would you expect him to come clean and report the mistake? We can all respect someone who tells us the truth and admits his or her mistake.

Or, would you expect him to hide the occurrence and avoid the embarrassment?

We cannot respect someone who does not tell the truth.
Let's continue on with our scenario:

> *You find out about the cover up when reviewing the records (he didn't quite wipe out all of the evidence). When you ask Bill about it, he tries to offer up excuses, "Well this happened, and that happened, and I did this, and it wasn't my fault."*

> *You choose to let it pass and let Bill's "CYA" excuses fly.*
> *You probably wouldn't do this for anyone else, but there's*
> *no real harm done, and Bill is your friend. Bill thanks*
> *you for helping him.*

The truth is – both of you know that Bill is being dishonest.

As the leader, if you allow Bill his excuse, you are now taking on his dishonesty, and dishonesty almost always leads to lost trust. You're making a personal choice to do the "comfortable" thing, rather than the right thing and you're treating Bill differently from others on the job because he's your friend.

What message does Bill get? What about the rest of your team? What will they think when they find out about what happened? (and there are no secrets really).

Will they be thinking, "It's OK to screw up as long as you're friends with the boss?"

Putting your own comfort or personal relationships first over the good of your team will lead to mistrust in the eyes of those who don't fall into the "privileged" group. Truthfully, even Bill will lose trust in you.

Significantly, in the case of the less-than-honest leader, an even deeper violation occurs in the minds of those who work for this person – a clear communication that when "push-comes-to-shove," their leader will save his or her own skin, or the skin of their friends, rather than be loyal to the team.

What else matters if a leader is not honest or acts without integrity? What good is the leader in the eyes of the team? What good is the leader who takes initiative, is fun to be around, or is a great communicator if the team can't count on that person?

Does all of this sound too idealistic for you? It's not.

Every great leader knows that a reputation of honesty and integrity is priceless.

When a leader acts without integrity, the team will pay the price, and that price will be very personal to them. The dishonorable leader will have placed a rock in the backpack of everyone else on their team. That extra burden of working for someone they don't trust will make every moment at work a just little harder for each of them.

So, at the core of every great leader lies this simple philosophy:

Honesty and Integrity Above All Else

Time management

Every leader - in fact every person - probably wishes they were better at time management.

One solution that works for many is a simple question. Ask yourself, "What is the most important use of my time right now?"

Ask it of yourself frequently and follow the answer without excuse. It's a simple question with powerful results for managing your time, effectively, and for all time!

Dealing with yourself

One true test of character is found in what a person does with their known shortfalls.

Be a better boss by addressing your own weaknesses and setting an example others can follow.

Endurance and tenacity

Consistently effective leadership takes discipline; the discipline of tenacity.

Be a better boss by steadfastly fighting any self-limiting urges you may have.

Procrastination, giving up, shying away from uncomfortable situations, or other ways of not staying the course are poison to your effectiveness and self-confidence.

Be a leader known for endurance and tenacity.

Subliminal or conscious leader?

As a new father, I vowed to avoid doing certain things that my parents had done. Strangely, I later found myself saying and doing exactly what I'd vowed I would not.

My parent's influence on me, subliminal in nature, was that strong!

As leaders, those we've worked for in the past may also have embedded strong subliminal messages within us.

Strengthen your leadership skills by trying to become consciously aware of your thoughts, words, and actions that are unwanted subliminal implants.

You can reprogram yourself to be a better leader and be true to what you believe when you understand the unconscious influences others may have had on you.

P to the sixth power

Proper Policies and Procedures Promote Productive Paradigms!

When we have to deal with a bad policy or procedure, it's like having a sore that won't heal; doubly so if we are told to just follow it and that it cannot be changed.

Then if your customers or other stakeholders get told things like, "We can't do this or that, even though it makes sense, because the policy says... (blah, blah, blah)," the resulting negative paradigm on both your staff and stakeholder can be deadly.

So make sure that every policy and procedure is effective, efficient, and productive.

Good leadership = good management = good paradigms!

And yes, there is another popular P^6: Proper Prior Planning Prevents Poor Performance. An oldie, but a goodie!

Leading the difficult

As leaders, we are expected to lead everyone in our charge effectively. That includes those who are difficult or who intimidate us.

Strengthen your team by thinking about how you are doing with those who are difficult for you to deal with.

Then talk to your boss, mentor(s), trusted peers – those you go to for wisdom – about how to be a more genuine leader for those difficult ones.

Help the more reflective people shine

Have you ever noticed, possibly in a meeting, that some people never seem to have an input when the group is asked for ideas?

One common reason is based on personality type, as in the Myers-Briggs Type Indicator® (MBTI)®. Some folks are naturally reflective and simply need more time to think things out. Their silence is really a matter of timing.

You can help them by asking these reflective types to think about their inputs a day or so before, and also by going back after the fact to ask them if they've had any further thoughts.

There is gold out there from reflective types if they are given time rather than being put on the spot, as too often happens.

How to be an assertive leader

Many leaders struggle with being assertive in the right way and at the right time. Consider this story:

> *My name is Tony and I run the customer service section at our local branch office. Last month our operations were being reviewed by a corporate team led by the Regional Office Manager. While he and I were going over our ISO-9001 processes, we were distracted by Sylvia, a senior member of my team, who was talking loudly with another worker. I personally find it difficult to deal with Sylvia. She intimidates me so I mostly try to stick to small*

talk and avoid crossing her.

The Regional Manager was annoyed with her loud voice. I prayed she would stop! When she didn't, he prodded me with a look to, "Go take care of that!"

With a lump in my throat, I approached and tried to quietly shush Sylvia. She looked at me with scorn and whispered, "Oh am I being too loud?" then went back to her conversation with a nasty glance back at me. I tried again and she ignored me. I'd had enough and thoughtlessly yelled "Shut up!" which is what the Regional Manager saw and heard as he walked up behind me.

He immediately took me into my office and had a formal counseling session with me about being disrespectful and too coercive, and directed me to apologize to Sylvia. How ironic and frustrating! I'm on the pad for being too hard, when I'm actually too passive! My future is in the toilet and I'm thinking of just quitting.

As with Tony, others will not respect and follow a leader who is too passive and lets others walk all over them. Being too passive can also lead to being indecisive, taking on work one shouldn't, or withholding vital information especially if it is bad news or unpopular. Too passive usually equals wimpy.

On the other hand, being too assertive is also hard for others to respect as it may leave them feeling pushed around, not listened to, manipulated, or dominated. Excessive assertiveness can also result in micro-management. Too assertive usually equals pushy, or even aggressive.

Interestingly, being too passive or too assertive both come from the same place in us as we unconsciously concentrate on the wrong thing - how we personally feel. Specifically we are operating from our comfort zone rather than thinking about and doing what is right for the team of people working for us. In both cases, the team knows this and loses respect and esprit-de-corps.

If this is you – too pushy or too passive – there are several things you can do to help apply these vital skills with the balance necessary to lead effectively.

First, consciously refocus yourself on doing what is right for your team instead of what makes you personally feel comfortable or avoiding discomfort.

Second, get a good mentor. Nothing is more effective at helping you deal with your shortfalls. Dissect past occurrences that went wrong, and then practice with your mentor the right way to think, act, and communicate. Also strategize with your mentor as new situations arise to fully retrain yourself and gain confidence with these skills.

Third, remain diligent at consciously focusing on doing what is right for your team instead of your personal comfort. There is strength for you in this higher purpose. Your team will respect that you've changed, after a time, and will come to know that you are out for them rather than yourself. This is leadership others can willingly support and follow.

Developing genuine leaders

Nearly everyone understands what being a genuine leader means.

However, it seems that many of today's leaders are little more than implementers of policy and procedure.

They have been asked too many times to check their brains at the door.

To fix this trend, senior leaders need to release the reins on their leadership team:

- Give them the power to act and tell you about it afterwards.

- Don't just give them the answers when questions arise; tell them to figure it out.

- Be far less accessible via phone, text, and email; let them feel the pressure of being in-charge.

By doing these kinds of things, you'll strengthen your current leaders and ensure that the next generation of leaders are strong ones!

Great bosses beget great bosses

It is a primary duty of every leader to develop their subordinates as leaders to ensure they are ready when opportunities arise.

While they can learn theory in many ways, the fine points (and that's what makes great bosses), can best be learned by tapping into the wisdom that you as the boss possess as you mentor them.

Be a better boss and give some real thought about exercising greater intent in developing those up-and-coming leaders who work for you.

ASK = Access Significant Knowledge

Once upon a time at a former workplace, a wonderful lady named

Sue used to work for me. She had worked there for over 30 years and had a record of darn near everything that had happened in that time, either in her head, in the computer, or even in hard copy in some cases. She had a vast historical knowledge.

Sue also had a great personality and honorable character. She related well to others and therefore had a vast knowledge of people too.

Early in our relationship, we developed a rapport of being open and honest with each other, which came to be invaluable to me as the leader. She used to come into my office and conduct what she called, "slap-therapy" sessions on me. In other words, she would tell me what I didn't know.

Sometimes it was from history, or who she knew. Sometimes it was from her professional knowledge. But in my recollection, the most meaningful times were when she would let me know how others were reacting to what I'd said or done – the impact of my actions.

As we got to know each-other better, she also became more proactive and kept me from saying or doing the wrong things and walking off a cliff.

Needless to say, I owe a lot to Sue for letting me "Access her Significant Knowledge." Thank you Sue!

Do you have a Sue in your life as a leader? All I can say is, if not, try to develop one to help you see your blind spots, like Sue did for me.

Planting an ASK person

Another way to utilize the ASK concept is to "plant" a person to feedback what they observe to you. What I used to do was plant someone to observe me and then tell me how I did. I used this at select times when I was holding team meetings, or talking to executive committees, etc.

What I learned was sometimes staggering. Things like, my facial expressions were all negative – I was "scrunchy-faced."

Again the most useful information I learned from this was the impact of my actions; how others felt and thought about what I said or did.

Source code

Last but not least, a significant ASK tool involves "source code," like in the movie Source Code (which I highly recommend BTW). The movie is based on the premise that each of us has an unconscious short-term memory of every minute detail that goes on around us, and this extends far beyond what we are aware of. The movie states that this is retained for about 8 minutes, and these short-term memories make up our "source code."

I don't know if I believe it as portrayed in the movie, but I do know from experience that the longer I wait after an event; the more likely I will forget details or "color" the events as I remember them.

What I like to do – and advocate to you now – is to seek out and get feedback ASAP after an event to take advantage of both your own and the other person's source code.

Wrapping it up

ASK = Access Significant Knowledge by developing a "Sue" in your life. When fully developed, this relationship can become proactive.

Plant an "ASK" person to observe you during an event and feedback their observations of your performance.

Access your own and others "source code" to find out things that might be missed if you wait.

Finally, I stayed away from saying the obvious as long as I could: The way to ASK is, of course, to ask!

The power of consistency

People work best when they have clarity.

The foundation of clarity rests in the team being able to count on who the leader is and what the leader stands for.

Lead with consistency and conscious intent. Minimize making things up as you go along.

When people can count on who you are and what you stand for, this consistency will build clarity and confidence on your team.

Act happier and smile more

"Have a lighthearted demeanor and easy-going spirit," said the best mentor I ever had. I wish I could say that I heeded those words of wisdom better - maybe most of us in management wish the same.

Be a more influential leader and lighten up. Act happier. Smile more.

Remove the heaviness from your speech, tone, and actions as much as you can. Doing this will remove some of the burden form those around you; peers, subordinates, or superiors.

The work will still get done, in better perspective and with more joy.

You have the power to make your team happier - and you'll be happier too!

Two key factors to building influence

It's easier to understand another person if we take the time to understand two things about them. Specifically, the differences between what they say, and why they are saying it.

What we say, do, or think = Our **Position**.

Why we say, do, or think something = Our **Interest**.

To use these to be stronger at influencing others;

1. Be slower in revealing your position and more diligent in revealing your interest.

2. Gain insight into others interest by observation and asking questions. Be sure to honor their interest; don't step on their toes in this regard.

Walk your talk

Does what you say match what you do? Have you promised to do things and not followed through as you should have?

People of high character, have high influence.

Look at the "inactive" items on your long-term to do list. Now pick the most significant item and move it to the top of your active list, then take action – even if it's tough or challenging. Doing what you say is integrity. Promises forgotten are in a broken state and are not.

Strengthen what you stand for and be sure to walk your talk. Use your influence for the good of your team.

Assertive Humility

We probably think of humility as being passive or submissive, but being a humble leader may mean an entirely different thing.

Rather than being meek or mild, the good leader must sometimes be humble by placing the needs of others above their own needs and wants. This can sometimes take an assertive form, such as when we need to provide feedback to someone about their poor performance.

We may fear a possible confrontation, but humility requires that we put our discomfort aside so that we can effectively tell the other person what they are doing wrong.

Be a better boss and be humble, especially in this very different, assertive way.

> *"True humility is not thinking less of yourself;*
> *it is thinking of yourself less." – C.S. Lewis*

Man-up

Male or female, we are at our finest as leaders when we "Man-up" at the proper time.

That starts by being a person of high character, with excellent integrity.

It then extends to taking personal responsibility for your own actions and for your team - especially when you're wrong.

Ultimately, manning-up involves exercising courage. The courage to act when fear grips you because taking action is the right thing to do. The courage of sacrifice to fight against wrongs and injustices - even when you "know" there is little hope of winning.

Be a better boss and decide to "Man-up" the next time you know you should.

Chapter Five

Leadership Zones

What is your current state of development as a leader and manager? Where has this brought you and your team?

Too many of us who are in leadership positions are frozen in time; our development arrested as we've settled into ways we find personally comfortable. The resulting team work climates produced are predictable.

These are not easy truths, and none of us are immune. It's very natural to settle in to what we find comfortable, even when it's wrong for those we lead.

Thank God that I found Howard, or rather that Howard found me, and decided to wake me from my coma.

For us to discuss how well-developed a leader is, we need a common language. To accomplish this, the concept of "Leadership Zones" provides a useful tool. It lets us discuss the state of development and the significant factors involved.

Consider the following story...

It was Tuesday and time for our weekly senior staff meeting. Paul, another longtime leader and friend, walked with me to the conference room. We both used to look forward to these meetings, but that enthusiasm has faded since our new company President took over six months ago.

The former company President, Ms. Hampton, was a strong purposeful leader whom everyone looked up to. When she was here we all worked hard and we sincerely felt like a team. She had high expectations, but also an involved and helpful nature. She knew what was going on and communications were open and meaningful. I could go on, but it's sufficient to say that Ms. Hampton was a solid leader, a view that I know was shared by all of us.

Our new President, Mr. Astor is a nice enough person, but not focused it seems. When he first arrived he made it clear that he knew we were an accomplished team, and that his style was predominately Laissez-Faire. He declared his hands-off approach would work well as we were a proven team and could all obviously operate best with very with little direction from the top. It sounded like a fair assessment and a good way to go... at first. Now, six months later, well, I don't know.

Our staff meetings now seem to last forever and little real work gets accomplished or decisions made. We waste a lot of time now dealing with micro-details while the big picture slips away, and that seems to be the order of the day – unaware.

We seem to have lost our way, as everyone has reverted to their own comfort zones. Loyalty to the team has steadily decreased, and the behavior of the senior staff is very confusing. Paul and I have talked about it many times. We agreed that now, instead of a good team, the senior staff had devolved into factions based on power, or so it appears.

Some leaders seem to want to control everything, like Robert Smith. It feels like he could care less how others are affected; and this from a man I would have called an involved team-player in the past.

Others on the senior staff have gone in the opposite direction and just given up it seems, deferring to "whatever."

And in one very surprising instance, I observed a senior staff member, John Noble, literally promise the world to the President, then complain to subordinates and do nothing!

Most depressing in all of this is that Mr. Astor seems to be clueless about what is happening, even after Paul and I went to see him. He just gave us some "mumbo-jumbo" about staff now being free to make the best choices rather than being confined by his involvement, and that others had told him they liked having the leash slackened.

My frustration is very high, and I've had more than one discussion with Paul about moving on to a company that is smart about whom they put in charge. But, well - I guess I'm just "venting" because I could never leave and throw my team to the dogs.

I've been successful at filtering this stuff and keeping my subordinate leaders and their teams on track, but it's well known that things are going downhill with the senior staff. This is starting to permeate throughout the company with great speed and negativity. Loyalty and respect are slipping away fast.

I wish there were something more Paul and I could do.

As with Mr. Astor in our story, we've all experienced people in positions of power who seem to have trouble understanding and using that power effectively. They appear to have settled into a personal zone of comfort which overrides their basic common sense and responsibility to those they lead.

But genuine leaders know that effective leadership lies outside their comfort zones. They challenge themselves to develop the skills they find difficult or which they are uneasy about, but which they know are necessary.

Challenging Your Zones of Discomfort

One of the best examples I've ever seen of a leader challenging his or her comfort zones occurred when I was in training to earn my MBTI® (Myers-Briggs Type Indicator®) certification.

After four days, our instructor asked us if we thought he was an introvert or an extrovert. Well it was obvious - he was an excellent instructor; engaging, dynamic, and energized by what he was doing. Clearly he was an extrovert.

We were all quite surprised when he disclosed himself to be an introvert!

In discussing this, the class concurred that being an instructor is certainly an extrovert-oriented skill. Significantly, the sharing of energy in a very external way is required to be an effective instructor, and this does not come naturally to an introvert, whose natural tendency is toward inward energy.

Our instructor had developed these extrovert-natural instructor skills because he was aware that it was necessary to consciously achieve a different comfort zone to be effective as an instructor. He had worked hard and had genuinely developed that comfort zone, so that to the outside observer, it looked natural.

However, because he is an introvert at heart – a fact that cannot be changed – his true natural comfort zone will always be inward and if he were not consciously aware of this, he might retreat to his natural comfort zone at the wrong time.

Now, this is unlikely when he's consciously in "instructor mode," but in the day-to-day world of leading a team; dealing with crisis and emotionally charged situations, the natural and unconscious tendency to go to your comfort zone and avoid your discomfort zones is much more pervasive and subtle.

The Importance of Awareness

To challenge our own comfort zones, a diligent awareness of the following is necessary:

1. Awareness of the situation and the dynamics as things change;

2. Awareness of self (strengths and weaknesses);

3. Awareness of how your areas of comfort and discomfort

affect your motivation and your actions;

4. Awareness of the impact of your actions; how others think and feel;

5. Awareness of non-tangibles; your gut feelings.

When you have true depth of awareness, you can stop operating in an unconscious, automatic way. In fact, that is the goal of the most effective leaders; to operate from awareness rather than from some subconscious, subliminal, habitual learned behavior.

Interestingly, research tells us that humans act from our subconscious most of the time. It all feels very right. We must then manufacture explanations for ourselves and others to justify our actions. Our natural way is to act first, think later, and then explain ourselves.

But effective leaders know that the reverse of our natural way works far better. First be aware; then think about the outcome we want; act with awareness; and evaluate the results.

Awareness is the central key to effective leadership.

True awareness is going to cause you discomfort because you must objectively own the results. But that is a good thing when you can use it to grow, unless you'd rather stick your...

Leadership vs. Management Skills

If awareness is a significant key to effectiveness, then the first thing to be aware of is that leadership skills are a unique skill-set. What it takes to lead others is not the same as managing processes and procedures.

Neither are the skills of leadership the same as technical or professional skills.

Yet it is common to see people advanced to supervisory positions based on their technical or professional skills rather than their ability to lead others.

Leadership is about influencing people, while management is about organization; process and procedure.

> *"You manage things; you lead people."*
> *- RADM Grace Hopper*

Many people in supervisory positions are excellent managers of policy, process, and procedure. They have highly developed skills in these areas. For many, these skills make up a comfort zone. After all, it's pretty natural to feel good about such things. But this is not leadership.

Leadership involves people. When we put people into the mix of policy, process, and procedure, the person in charge needs good leadership skills in order to influence others to follow them.

Influencing others is the end game of leadership; therefore leadership skills are required in some measure at every level, from CEO down to one worker being tasked to train another worker. Likewise, good management skills are needed at every level.

That brings us to a question:

*I*s it possible to be a good manager, but a poor leader?

The answer is yes. We've probably all seen this in action; someone who manages things well but who is a poor leader. In fact, it's all too common, isn't it?

What about the reverse then?

*C*an you be a good leader, but a poor manager?

The answer is No. Both leadership and management skills are required to be a good leader. In fact, good management skills are a vital part of the leadership skill set.

A leader who lacks proper management skills is not fully efficient and therefore not fully effective.

As an example, consider what it's like to follow a leader who is disorganized. The fact that the leader is disorganized will influence the team in negative ways. That negative influence is something a genuine leader will not allow.

Or, consider what it's like to work for a leader who constantly violates policies or procedures because they are poorly written or out of date. A genuine leader would not allow this as a matter of routine, and work to get them corrected or updated.

In order to be a fully effective, genuine leader, you must therefore also be a fully effective manager.

The Importance of Focus

Let's start our discussion of focus with a question:

Where do we humans naturally focus our attention and effort?

You have 5 seconds to answer... 3 – 2 – 1, time's up!

Our natural focus is of course, on ourselves. We naturally look out for ourselves, to varying degrees, in every situation.

In a useful sense, it's why we are attuned to avoid rocks flying at our heads, and why we instinctively swerve our car to avoid a deer running into our path.

When coupled with a healthy sense of responsibility, it's also why we resist injustice and fight for fairness.

But, we all know about the "dark side of the force." Self-centeredness as a primary motive; concern for others very low or non-existent.

If a leader acts in this self-centered way, they are labeled as "Out for #1, "and no one wants to work for a leader who is, "Out for themselves."

Sadly, some of us are that leader.

On the other hand, we all know where genuine leaders focus their efforts. They do what is right, even when it's hard for them to do so. They stand up for their team, even if they personally lose. Everyone wants to work for a leader like that.

Focus is a primary consideration for us as we now look at leadership zones.

The Leadership Zones

There are three Leadership Zones which are categorized by two primary factors:

1. The level of awareness the leader possesses and;
2. Their focus:
   a. Outward toward what others need; the team.
   b. Inward; focused on self first.

The following gives an overview of each of the three zones:

Zone 1	Zone 2	Zone 3
- Fully Aware - Focused on others first - Fully Effective - Genuine Leader	- Fully Aware - Focused on self first - Effectiveness limited by self-centered focus - Disingenuous Leader	- Awareness and/or focus are unsteady; influenced by stress, pressure, emotions, and situations - Effectiveness is erratic - Unstable Leader

Zone 1: The Zone 1 leader is operating in a highly effective zone of comfort. They are not perfect; they make mistakes, but are aware of the impact of their actions.

Zone 1 leaders focus outward; doing what is right for the team over what is right for them personally.

They are constantly perfecting themselves as leaders

and managers. They are open to changing as necessary to ensure their actions are in the best interest of the team, the organization, and customers.

Zone 2: The Zone 2 leader is fully aware of their shortfalls and the impact of their actions.

Zone 2 leaders focus inward on themselves first. Because of this focus, they are intentionally limiting their leadership effectiveness.

Many Zone 2 leaders are stuck in habits or hung up in some significant way and are choosing to stay in their comfort zone rather than do what is right for the team, the organization, or their customers.

Zone 3: The Zone 3 leader has an unsteady awareness and / or focus.

Their focus and awareness tend to shift as influenced by stress, pressure, or various other forces. They are capricious; mercurial.

When their focus or awareness shifts, they tend to be acutely aware of this shift. But in fairness, they may be only somewhat aware of the full impact of their actions.

Their unsteady awareness and/or focus cause their effectiveness to be erratic.

There are a great many distinct forms and variations of Zone 3 leadership, as many as there are leaders who get it wrong.

Key Points of Chapter Five

1. Leadership skills are a unique skill-set, different from other skills such as technical or professional skills.

2. Leaders may settle into zones of comfort, or zones that avoid discomfort. While either of these may seem personally correct, they can be destructive if they are not also right for the team.

3. Leadership is about influencing people, while management is about organization; process and procedure.

4. Zone 1 leaders are fully effective genuine leaders.

5. Zone 1 leadership skills can be developed as we acknowledge our limitations and use them to our advantage.

Chapter Six

Zone 1 Leaders

Zone 1	Zone 2	Zone 3
- Fully Aware - Focused on others first - Fully Effective - Genuine Leader	- Fully Aware - Focused on self first - Effectiveness limited by self-centered focus - Disingenuous Leader	- Awareness and/or focus are unsteady; influenced by stress, pressure, emotions, and situations - Effectiveness is erratic - Unstable Leader

The Zone 1 leader is operating in a highly effective zone of comfort. They are not perfect; they make mistakes, but are aware of the impact of their actions.

Zone 1 leaders focus outward; doing what is right for the team over what is right for them personally.

They are constantly perfecting themselves as leaders and managers and are open to changing as necessary to ensure their actions are in the best interest of the team, the organization, and customers.

Understanding Zone 1 Leadership

So, what is a Zone 1 leader? What makes a leader fully effective and genuine? Consider the following story...

> *My name is Susan Rodgers. I lead the project management group for our company's operations in the mid-west. We recently received a highly visible and politically sensitive project. My group was tasked with coordinating all efforts of the company nationwide, as well as sub-contractors and government oversight elements. This was a great opportunity for us and the company, and our reputation and future opportunities for the firm were definitely on the line. As they say, with great opportunity comes great risk. Accordingly, I took the time to really think this out before I briefed my team.*

> *On Monday I gathered them together. I began to draw an outline of how I saw the project unfolding, and after a couple of minutes, Bill Carnegie, one of my senior planners raised his hand. "Boss, we've been through a lot of projects and I think we really know what we're doing. How about if you leave and let the rest of us plan this one. We'll come and get you when we're ready to present it to you."*

> *I stopped and said, "Give me a minute. "*

>> *I thought to myself... Well the team is very senior and they do have decades of technical experience, that is except for Andrea and Kelly, but the senior folks could make sure they are included. On the other hand, this might be risky. All the home office executives will be watching this one VERY*

closely, but then the team knows that. Can I trust them? Yes, of course, and after all, they are asking me for this, what more could I want as a leader? Besides, I will have the final say and we have time. Why not?

"Okay, that sounds good," I said. Just to be clear, we need the final plan done by this Friday, so I'll need to go over it with you a day or two ahead of time. Does Wednesday at 1:00 P.M. work for everyone's schedule?" The team all agreed except Allen who had a conflicting deadline, but he said he'd adjust it as this project took precedence.

"One more thing," I said. "Andrea and Kelly are still in training and I want to make sure they learn all they can from this, so for you senior folks, please be sure that happens." Bill Carnegie said, "Consider it done - any other questions or concerns boss?"

"No, you've got the football, have fun!" I left the room confident that things would go well.

What happened during this meeting may seem a little benign at first glance. That tends to be the nature of Zone 1 leadership - on target with everything fitting well. Clearly Susan was indeed fully effective and genuine with her team being the same. The team is indeed a reflection of her leadership.

Another way to look at this is by thinking about what could have happened if Susan were not a Zone 1 leader. There are a thousand ways she could have blown it. She could have been overly concerned with her own reputation and insisted on micro-managing things. She could have set deadlines without asking what worked or allowing any flexibility. We can all probably think of other ways we've seen leaders fail.

In that regard, Zone 1 leaders stand apart in that they consciously develop themselves toward making fewer and fewer mistakes. They strive to make each mistake only once, correct it, and then grow from it.

So the answer to our question, "What is a Zone 1 leader?" is somewhat ethereal in that there is no list of right and wrong to go by. Rather, Zone 1 leaders have the ability and flexibility to read and react to what is right for the team as things develop. They are not stuck in any pre-conceived box, rather, their box changes as the shape of things change. But, they always have things in the box, not out of control.

As you and I work with Zone 1 leaders, we may come to think of them as "natural leaders," instead of those who developed their leadership traits with intention. Let's take a look at this notion and the differences between the natural and the developed leader.

Natural vs. Developed Leader

From early childhood and throughout their formative years, the natural leader has had their leadership traits ingrained in them. Their parents and other influential individuals mentored them with openness and honesty, so that the values and traits they possess seem quite natural and even intrinsic to them.

So-called "natural leaders" are guided by a value system that supports understanding the personal and interpersonal aspects of their actions as they relate to the greater service of others. They are perceived as being totally honest and trustworthy.

They seem to naturally think in terms of what is right for the team they are a part of, as this is their personal preference. They lead from any position they find themselves in, never limited by title, pay grade, or official rules.

Decision making and effectively communicating the course of action they decide upon is so clear to the natural leader that everyone tends to quickly get behind it. Others tend to mirror and aspire to act in the same decisive way.

However, the natural leader is not perfect. They engage in constant self-assessment and feedback to ensure maximum effectiveness and growth in order to hone their skills. In other words, there actually is a developmental aspect essential to the so-called "natural leader."

The developed leader, on the other hand, consciously decides to develop their leadership values and traits. This does not come naturally and is frequently sparked by a need growing out of a significant event or events in their lives. In other words, when the errors they make become significant enough, the need to develop becomes obvious to them they push themselves to take action.

Lacking the elemental framework that the natural leader possesses, the developed leader must work consciously so that they start to think as the natural leader does. This journey is not an easy one for most. It is a constant push and pull of emotions, habits and ideas which plague one to revert to what they did before.

When the developed leader has achieved their goal of thinking and behaving like the natural leader, the differences between them become indistinguishable to others. They are both equally effective which is why developed leaders may look like natural leaders to others.

Their different paths to success are immaterial; both natural and developed Zone 1 leaders are fully effective genuine leaders.

Zone 1 Leaders Focus on Others

In leadership as in all other things, we excel at certain aspects and have weaknesses in other areas. It is likely that we feel very comfortable and confident in doing what we excel at, and likewise less confident, uncomfortable, and unsure when doing what we feel weaker at. These zones of comfort and discomfort exist in every leader. How we deal with them defines us as leaders.

As leaders, choosing to lead from our comfort zones is fundamentally self-centered. Zone 1 leaders do not allow themselves to do this. Instead, they understand that the very cornerstone of honorable leadership is to serve those they lead, and overcome their weaknesses and flaws to do so.

The difference that makes these leaders effective is that when faced with taking action that is personally uncomfortable, they push through their discomfort and do what is right rather than choosing self first.

Selfless service is a hallmark of being a genuine leader; a Zone 1 leader.

Key Points of Chapter Six

1. Both natural and developed leaders operate in Zone 1 as fully effective genuine leaders.

2. Zone 1 leaders make fewer and fewer mistakes as they continually develop. They strive to make each mistake only once, correct it, and then grow from it.

3. Zone 1 leaders have the ability to read and react to what is right for the team as things develop. They are not stuck in any pre-conceived box.

4. In order to be a fully effective Zone 1 leader, you must also be a fully effective manager.

5. Selfless service is a hallmark of being a genuine leader; a Zone 1 leader.

Chapter Seven
Zone 2 Leaders

Zone 1	Zone 2	Zone 3
- Fully Aware - Focused on others first - Fully Effective - Genuine Leader	- Fully Aware - Focused on self first - Effectiveness limited by self-centered focus - Disingenuous Leader	- Awareness and/or focus are unsteady; influenced by stress, pressure, emotions, and situations - Effectiveness is erratic - Unstable Leader

The Zone 2 leader is fully aware of their shortfalls and the impact of their actions.

Zone 2 leaders focus inward; on themselves first. Because of this focus, they are intentionally limiting their leadership effectiveness.

Many Zone 2 leaders are stuck in habits or hung up in some significant way and choose to stay in their comfort zone rather than do what is right for the team, the organization, or their customers.

Three Examples of Zone 2 Leaders

The *"Self-Disabled"* leader typifies Zone 2 leaders. They are stuck in behaviors that feel comfortable for them, though this may be wrong for their team and the organization as a whole. They may be very effective in some, or even many situations, but highly ineffective in others as a result of their personal needs overriding what they know to be proper leadership behavior.

Most perplexing is that some of these self-disabled leaders are comfortable in their inability because they are not held accountable; they have no fear of ramifications. The self-disabled can recover from this with structure, accountability, and mentoring to become Zone 1 leaders.

There are a small number of *"Imposed Upon"* Zone 2 leaders; those who've tried to change but have come up against actual inabilities within themselves. Certain necessary leadership functions are exceptionally difficult for them to perform. This is not by choice, rather they do not have these functions in them nor can they be developed.

They should not have been advanced to leadership in the first place, and should be allowed to return to another job where they can be effective. The demands of leadership will take a human toll on such a person. Unfortunately, many organizations will not allow voluntary demotion, only having an "up or out" policy.

Last, are Zone 2 leaders that we'll call *"Out for #1"* leaders. They know the right answers and fake proper leadership behavior, while actually staying in their zone of comfort.

They look like fully effective leaders but this is only a front they put on for higher-ups. Therefore, higher-ups incorrectly see them as

Zone 1 leaders. Their team knows the real person they are and knows they are out for themselves first.

The "Out for #1" leader can recover from this, but may only be able to change if a Zone 1 higher-up takes the time to confront the truth with them, using documented accountability, developmental plans, mentoring and supervisory involvement. They can become Zone 1 leaders but they have the toughest hill to climb – confronting their true self with courage to change who they essentially are.

Let's take a closer look at each of the three manifestations of Zone 2 leaders.

The "Self-Disabled" Zone 2 Leader

We have all experienced supervisors who know the right answers, but sometimes do the wrong things. This is puzzling because during those times, it is very obvious that these "Self-disabled" leaders are more concerned with their personal comfort or security over what they know to be proper leadership action. But for them, knowing and doing are two distinctly different things, with their needs usually winning out.

This need for personal comfort and security generally manifests itself in two ways. "Self-disabled" leaders either take action they know is wrong, or through fear, avoid acting when they know they should.

For instance, a leader may be disorganized and habitually late, wasting everyone's time. They are somehow content in their tardiness, and rather than change, they may laugh this off and tell others something like, "You know how I am!"

Typical for many "Self-disabled" leaders, the areas in which they demonstrate their misplaced motivations are very specific, yet they can be highly effective otherwise.

For example, consider Jack – a team leader of four surveyors marking out a new flood control channel in the New Orleans area:

> *I (Jack) was so excited when I was put in charge of this team. We would be operating for months out in the back country on a very important and politically sensitive new project.*
>
> *Throughout the preliminary planning stages I was happier than I'd been in years; finally being able to get back to the field work I loved. You see, I was "promoted" five years ago to what essentially amounted to working on my own in a cube in the corner doing Quality Assurance. Now I was going to lead a team again and get muddy!*
>
> *Then I found out who was on my team and my heart sank. Jill Smith, or "Ornery Jill" as I like to think about her. She shows me no respect and refuses to do what I ask of her.*
>
> *A week ago I timidly tried to tell her to do something, and she got angry and meanly grunted, "Make me!" in front of the rest of the team.*
>
> *Now I barely see her and I really don't know what she's up to. Frankly I'm happy to have it that way – except – well, I am supposed to be in charge and responsible for what we accomplish. But what can I do? I'm just no good at confrontation.*

Hopefully Jill is doing something productive, but if not, I'm sure the rest of us will be able to fill in the gaps. At least the rest of the team works!

Jack is an effective leader with those who only need to be managed. But for those who need a genuine leader, like Jill and those on the team that she is a part of, Jack is ineffective because he is more concerned with his own comfort than leading them.

Instead of dealing with Jill's insubordination, which is the right thing for his team, he allowed her to walk all over him. The rest of the team suffers for his inaction. Jill is also not doing well under his "Self-disabling" behavior. Her performance and job satisfaction are also part of Jack's responsibility, but the team and Jill are far from Jack's mind.

Sometimes a "Self-disabled" leader like Jack will talk openly about their shortfalls and their inability to change. As they describe it, they are somehow being victimized by their strong comfort and security needs. They feel quite powerless over them and lean on these to justify their behavior.

The "Imposed Upon" Zone 2 Leader

Leaders who are "Imposed Upon" do have an accurate awareness of their weaknesses and recognizing the need to change. They have likely spent many futile hours seeking help and advice to try to find the right answer or technique that will resolve their inability to effectively do what they know they should. This is very frustrating as they try very hard, but just can't make things work for them. Consider the following:

My name is Walt and I hate my job.

I would do anything to go back to my old desk. I've tried everything, but I just can't seem to get it right when it comes to getting others to work for me. They don't do what I tell them, and I end up having to step in and do things myself just to meet deadlines. It's very obvious to me that they don't respect me.

I always thought that it would be great to be a supervisor. My father retired from the Air Force and is still to this day a recognized leader. My sister Alice is a lawyer for a multi-national corporation and leads a team of other lawyers working on environmental compliance. But unlike them, I just don't seem to have inherited the leadership gene.

I do have a mentor who I've been working with for the last six months. My boss also goes out of her way to try to help me. I've tried everything they suggested to no end.

Things are always fairly cordial; after all I used to be just another worker here before I was advanced. But now when I try to shift and be the leader, I immediately feel the discomfort. I feel like a mouse, totally gun shy.

My mentor and boss have both told me that I need to be firmer and more direct; that I sound too suggestive rather than giving clear direction. But every time I try, it comes out wrong.

It's eating my heart out. Confidentially I've stopped trying and just do the work myself to avoid beating myself up in front of my co-workers, I mean team members. I'm getting here earlier than ever and staying late, and my wife is pushing me hard to stop doing that. I feel like I'm aging faster and I just want to quit, but I still have twelve years to go until retirement.

I have asked to be allowed to go back to my old job, but my boss immediately told me that wasn't an option, and that I just needed to stick with it until I get it right. Nobody hears me, I swear. Oh, why did I ever take this job!

Does this sound like anyone you know or have ever known? Think of how much energy is being wasted trying to put Walt's square peg into a round hole.

The same people who advanced Walt without ensuring that he would have the skills and abilities he needs to lead are now telling him the decision is final. Clearly they are not Zone 1 leaders, and may also be "self-disabled" Zone 2 leaders.

They either knew, or at least now know, what is wrong with Walt, but are unwilling to effectively lead in this situation by doing what is right for both Walt and the team he leads.

Think about that for a minute. Clearly Walt is not an effective leader and this is not good for those he is in charge of, but the mentor and his boss just keep trying to fix Walt while the team continues to go downhill.

Remember...

Every time you see a failing leader that is not being helped effectively, you are actually seeing at least two failing leaders, because it is the higher-up leader's responsibility to make sure their subordinate leaders are effective.

The "Out for #1" Zone 2 Leader

A while back, a leader at a company we were working with walked up to me in the hall and told me that she was being promoted to a national leadership position. I congratulated her heartily as she told me the details and how hard she'd worked to get the promotion. It was impressive to say the least.

A few moments later, I came across two of her subordinate leaders that I'd worked with in the past. I mentioned that she'd told me about her promotion and how impressive her efforts sounded to me.

They looked at each other and rolled their eyes. Then one of them grabbed my upper arm, pulled me close and whispered something like,

> *"Bob, just between us, she got that promotion by stepping all over the rest of us. She always makes sure she looks good and has hung us out to dry so many times that we've lost count. She's horrible, and let me tell you, we are all very happy she's leaving."*

What a tragedy. This is not the right leader for a national position as her impact was now going to be much broader and affect far more people.

The leaders who selected her failed to do their job and have now advanced someone they shouldn't have. The irony is that there were many others below her level who knew the truth. It is also quite likely her peers and immediate supervisor knew the truth about her. So why didn't this information make it to the right ears?

There are many reasons that the truth about poor leadership

performance doesn't come to light with higher-ups, but one particular factor is almost always at play; the higher-ups created a climate which favored keeping such things a secret and in the end, didn't ask the right people in the right way.

Now she has been advanced to an even higher level of incompetence.

Again, every time you see a failing leader that is not being helped effectively, you are actually seeing at least two failing leaders, because it is the higher-up leader's responsibility to make sure their subordinate leaders are effective.

Shifting Zones

Emotions being emotions, we'd all like to think that we are in Zone 1 a majority of the time and that we shift to one of the other zones on occasion.

Zone 2 leaders are especially prone toward feeling that they are in Zone 1 most of the time, and "slip" into Zone 2 occasionally. In actuality, this is justification for their self-centered focus. They are attempting to minimize and make it seem like it's not that bad in the full light of day.

True Zone 1 leaders have their moments of being self-centered too; they are human after all. But they acknowledge this as being improper, correct anything that happened as a result, and work to eliminate this kind of behavior.

Putting our emotions aside, realize that Zone 1 is an absolute; you are either there, or you are not.

Key Points of Chapter Seven

1. Zone 2 leaders are fully aware of their weaknesses.

2. Every time you see a failing leader that is not being helped effectively, you are actually seeing at least two failing leaders, because it is the higher-up leader's responsibility to make sure their subordinate leaders are effective.

3. Zone 2 leaders may want to see themselves as being Zone 1 except for having some shortfalls. But this is not valid in reality because part time effectiveness is simply not the same as being a genuine leader.

4. Zone 1 leaders are genuine leaders and do not shift back and forth from other zones.

Chapter Eight

Zone 3 Leaders

Zone 1	Zone 2	Zone 3
- Fully Aware - Focused on others first - Fully Effective - Genuine Leader	- Fully Aware - Focused on self first - Effectiveness limited by self-centered focus - Disingenuous Leader	- Awareness and/or focus are unsteady; influenced by stress, pressure, emotions, and situations - Effectiveness is erratic - Unstable Leader

The Zone 3 leader has an unsteady awareness and / or focus.

Their focus and awareness tend to shift as influenced by stress, pressure, or various other forces. They are capricious and mercurial.

When their focus or awareness shifts, they tend to be acutely aware of this shift. But in fairness, they may be only somewhat aware of the full impact of their actions.

Their unsteady awareness and/or focus cause their effectiveness to be erratic.

There are a great many distinct forms and variations of Zone 3 leadership, as many as there are leaders who get it wrong.

Zone 3 leaders usually have a limited awareness of their shortfalls and are only somewhat aware of the full impact of their actions. Their ability to change is a "shot in the dark" because they do not have an accurate understanding of what or how to change.

However, some Zone 3 leaders are open to changing and are actively working to develop into Zone 1 leaders.

Sometimes a Zone 3 leader will have learned a tactic from other leaders and will attempt to simply follow what they have learned. However, because they lack a deep understanding of why this works, they are unable to generalize what they know or adapt it in a consistent way as events require.

Occasionally a Zone 3 leader can "Copycat" others effectively enough to look like a more developed leader, but because they have no real understanding, they are lost when there is no effective model to follow. "Copycat" activity is usually reactionary "tunnel-vision." It is a way of dealing with limited awareness. The hope is self-preservation.

Zone 3 "tunnel-vision" may also be a result of an intentional act by the leader, an intentional denial of information by others, or an actual limitation of the individual's abilities.

The Bottom Line on Zone 3

The bottom line is that Zone 3 leaders are confusing to work for and usually cannot be counted on because of their unsteadiness and changeability.

I know this very well because I was a Zone 3 leader for a long time.

Consider the nameplate story in Chapter One; what Howard meant when he said, *"Bob, if you have no idea who you are or what you are all about, then your team won't be able to count on you, and will have no confidence in you."*

Being a Zone 3 leader can be a scary place because you may feel like you're walking on the edge of a cliff, which leads you to taking whatever action you can to keep from falling off.

This means you'll be a leader who is blown with the four winds, and your team along with you.

The Interim Leader

When a leadership position is left unfilled for some time, or "gapped" as it is sometimes called, it is commonplace to find someone to take on this position in an "interim" status, sometimes as a collateral duty.

Who is chosen is critical to the team. If the interim is a Zone 1 leader, they will act in an effective manner until the new permanent leader arrives, which is of course what the team and the organization desire.

However, if the interim is a Zone 2 "Self-disabled" or "Imposed upon" leader, or if they happen to be in Zone 3, they could easily treat this assignment in the wrong way, such as seeing this assignment as a bother, or more likely, approaching it with fear.

Or, if the interim is a Zone 2 "out-for-#1" leader, they may either see this as hindering their image with higher-ups, or as an opportunity to leverage it for their own benefit.

In any case, none of the attitudes that these Zone 2 or Zone 3 leaders bring to this assignment are desirable for the team. The evidence of this is what you and I have clearly heard from interims on many occasions, such things as, "I'm only here for emergencies," or "I'm only the interim and I'm not going to change anything or make any decisions unless I have to."

Or the clearly Zone 3 speech, "I don't have much time, so I'll be at my regular desk and I'll check in from time-to-time. Don't get a hold of me unless it's really important. I'm sure you (the team) can handle all the routine stuff."

These types of statements guarantee that the interim will be operating as a Zone 3 leader in relation to filling this temporary position because they have created a "tunnel vision" environment for themselves. Interestingly, many around them (except for Zone 1 leaders), especially higher-ups, will treat their ignorance with an understanding attitude; after all, they are only there on a temporary basis.

One thing this commonly produces for the team is created crises. The Zone 3 interim makes them jump through hoops to make up for his or her lack of awareness, especially when higher-ups push the interim for information or action from the team.

This underscores the main problem – what about the team? If the team was included as a primary consideration, then those choosing the interim leader would only have one choice – install a Zone 1 leader.

From Zone 3 to Zone 1

As we previously observed, the main issue with being a Zone 3 leader stems from shifting awareness or focus. In many real world instances, this results in the leader taking ineffective or inappropriate action. This undermines the Zone 3 leader's ability to lead as the team comes to see them as inept.

This is not an unrecoverable position, and the Zone 3 leader can develop toward Zone 1 leadership, but only with the help of a solid Zone 1 mentor who can open their eyes.

Other Zone 3 leaders have advanced to their position based on technical skills or seniority and therefore have a strong belief in their own competence. This illusionary self-confidence carries over to their leadership abilities as they are functionally unaware of their shortfalls. They believe they are effective leaders and as a result have little motivation to further develop.

This belief can be so strong that it limits their ability to receive feedback about their performance. They may look with puzzlement at another who is trying to tell them about their performance, shrug them off, and return to their comfort zone. They think that the other individual is the one who doesn't get it. They believe their actions to be those of an effective leader and see their actions as doing what is best for the team; after all, they know best and are right in their own perception.

This type of leader is likely to have the most difficulty understanding their shortcomings and resist making the transition to move toward Zone 1. They will likely require a very strong, mature, and senior Zone 1 leader to be their mentor as this process of change for the Zone 3 leader will probably involve numerous repetitive reinforcements.

Please consider the following story...

Bryce Phillips was a student in a year-long senior leadership development program I conducted. Bryce was certainly a "wise acre." For instance; he claims that he was actually born on the electrical maintenance shop floor. He started there 32 years ago right out of school and this is the only company he has ever worked for. He started out sweeping the floor and learned what he could here and there from the electricians doing maintenance. He eventually worked himself up to a point where the company sent him to trade school, and after 20 years of hard work, he became the head of electrical repair and maintenance.

I remember the first time he spoke in class. He was absolutely forthright as he exclaimed that being there was a waste of time for him and that the people who sent him should know that. Still, he couldn't help speaking up in class from time-to-time when the discussion happened to align with his personal views. But for the vast majority of the first 4 or 5 classes, he just sat there, arms crossed looking straight ahead.

Somewhere around that point in time, I visited Bryce's department to work with his team de-briefing the results of their organizational climate survey. The idea was to have them work together as a team and set goals to improve the way they did things as a team. However, this didn't quite happen.

The whole discussion seemed thwarted and little was accomplished. Afterward, one of the senior team members pulled me aside and explained that, "Nothing good will come from that discussion. We can never speak our minds without making sure it's in line with what Bryce wants."

His control was near absolute. If he liked you and you did everything his way, including saying what he wanted to hear, then all was well. If you crossed him in any way, and this was extremely easy, you could find yourself ostracized, and he always got rid of those he didn't like.

Another part of the development program involved our conducting individual coaching sessions with each of the participants. During these, I consistently challenged Bryce's ways, ideas, paradigms, and the results they had on team climate and performance. The results of these discussions were also reported to Bryce's supervisor.

Bryce's supervisor Karen took this as an opportunity to try to change things for the better. Frankly, I know that Bryce didn't make it easy for her, to say the least. But she was trying.

Six months later, the program ended, and I found out what we had accomplished with Bryce. As I was leaving the building he pulled up in his car. He put his hand out the window for me to shake and told me that he was impressed. He had been so sure that there was nothing I could teach him, but then he admitted that he had, "Learned a thing or two." For him, this was a huge admission.

We talked for about 30-minutes, a conversation that ended with this final glimmer of hope that he really wanted to change; he told me that he would make a real effort to listen better as he saw the benefits for himself and his team.

Checking back six months later, Bryce had been true to his word. His supervisor was still chipping away at his attitude and ways of doing things that are deeply imbedded in Zone 3.

Things had improved for his team and everyone else as he was a better listener and somewhat more open to other's ideas.

Hope Won't Fix Bad Attitudes

We have all probably seen training thrown at a performance issue in an attempt to correct deep-rooted negative attitudes.

Or we've watched a leader, even an upper-level leader, wait for a bad apple to retire rather than dealing with them effectively.

Leaders who make such decisions are usually more concerned with their own comfort than doing what is right for the team.

Everyone on the team knows that the "problem person" is not being dealt with effectively. This undermines the team. It also makes it painfully obvious that the leader is weak.

Unfortunately, hope won't fix bad attitudes.

Zone 1 leaders don't rely on hope. They act to salvage every person they can to build a stronger team. Rather than fire, retire, or re-assign, they deal with these issues by exercising leadership influence. This could involve many different courses of action, but central to any solution would be effective performance counseling and mentoring.

Predictably, Zone 3 leaders are probably incapable of doing this type of mentoring effectively. They are more likely to deal with their problem people by trying to manage them away and hope this works.

And again, hope won't fix bad attitudes.

Key Points of Chapter Eight

1. Care needs to be taken when choosing who to put in charge, whether in an interim situation or as part of the regular selection process. Zone 3 leaders are usually a poor choice and the team will usually suffer for it.

2. Zone 3 leaders can develop themselves into Zone 1, with proper assistance and mentoring from a Zone 1 leader.

3. Zone 3 leaders are frequently in a very scary place, and so may be very open to changing.

Chapter Nine

Team Working Climate

Zone 1	Zone 2	Zone 3
- Fully Aware - Focused on others first - Fully Effective - Genuine Leader	- Fully Aware - Focused on self first - Effectiveness limited by self-centered focus - Disingenuous Leader	- Awareness and/or focus are unsteady; influenced by stress, pressure, emotions, and situations - Effectiveness is erratic - Unstable Leader

The team working climate of an organization tends to mirror the Zone make up of the leadership team.

Individual teams within the organization may have a different climate than the company as a whole, again based on the Zone make up of the leaders.

Let's look at each of these working climates individually and what it's like to work in them.

Zone 1 Team Working Climate

When the preponderance of leaders are Zone 1, the working climate of the organization is highly effective and it becomes a very desirable place to work.

Zone 1 leaders and organizations primarily concentrate on facts.

Things work well in nearly all areas, and Zone 1 leaders tend to have an excellent understanding of one-another's roles and the impact throughout the organization. This allows them to make well-informed decisions based on an accurate consideration of their impact, including second and third order effects.

The Zone 1 climate is a direct reflection of the dominance of the Zone 1 leaders.

Zone 1 leaders are very clear and direct in their expectations. They remain flexible to changing as necessary around the point of reaching the organization's goals. They are not emotionally tied to any particular idea or course of action; rather they want to do what is most effective. They embrace the concept of being forward-looking through the process of collaboration and barrier-free communication.

Zone 1 organizations utilize praise and constructive criticism in a balanced approach. Destructive criticism has no place in a Zone 1 organization, and those who use it are quickly mentored toward understanding its effect and making their criticisms constructive instead.

A high degree of loyalty and respect is felt throughout the entire operation. No one needs to take charge of morale as everyone is part of it, and it is quite high. People willingly take more initiative in Zone 1 organizations as a result of this.

Within a Zone 1 organization, new hires tend to also be Zone 1. Zone 1 hiring managers and committees are drawn to hiring Zone 1 candidates. They are also adept at identifying Zone 2 and 3 types and excluding them on that basis. Additionally, Zone 1 candidates are drawn to Zone 1 leaders and organizations and they tend to not accept offers from Zone 2 or 3 companies. Indeed, Zone 1 leaders are the only group having a good handle on assessing leadership skills in others as a separate skill set required for success in leading others.

Zone 1 leaders have a great understanding of others, and they use this effectively with leaders who are in Zones 2 and 3 to help them develop into better leaders with an eye toward moving them into Zone 1.

Zone 1 leaders do not fire employees without exhausting every option possible to allow others to correct shortfalls and develop, therefore, when someone has to be let go, it is the employee who decided not to develop themselves who really made the choice to leave.

The primary key to becoming and remaining a Zone 1 leader is an effective system of mentoring.

Zone 1 organizations view formal mentoring systems as vital, so for an organization to be at Zone 1, they must have a formal mentoring system in place at every level of the organization. In a Zone 1 workplace this just seems natural as everyone is openly expecting great feedback (praise and constructive criticism), coaching, and guidance.

To enhance awareness, Zone 1 mentoring typically uses formal feedback tools such as assessments and surveys. Mentors and mentees actively use these to set specific leadership development goals.

Accountability in Zone 1 Organizations

Zone 1 organizations place emphasis on appropriate responsibility and accountability including proper grading and documentation in their performance evaluation system.

In a Zone 1 climate, Zone 1 leaders welcome this. On the other hand, Zone 2 and 3 leaders may initially view this as punitive; however this is not the intent of honest and accurate grading in a Zone 1 climate.

Supervisors and mentors recognize this and work to ensure that Zone 2 and 3 leaders view accurate performance evaluation grades and comments as important checks and balances to keep them on track toward development. This is admittedly a fine balancing act to ensure that proper evaluation grades or comments are not perceived as punishment; good or bad, they are earned and it is proper and fair that evaluations reflect this.

Another significant paradigm in Zone 1 organizations is acceptance of the fact that leaders at all levels are responsible for the leadership performance and development of all subordinate leaders who work for them.

The senior leader is accountable for this in their evaluations, and this includes any mismatch between the grades they assign subordinate leaders and the results of those leader's feedback surveys, climate surveys, or other evaluating instruments.

In other words, if a subordinate leader's evaluation grades don't reflect the feedback their team provides, the senior leader is accountable and this lack of leadership will be included in their performance evaluation.

Zone 1 Team Working Climate Summary

The Zone 1 team working climate is marked by openness and honesty at its core. Zone 1 leaders are not perfect, but they work to correct issues as they become aware of them and expect the same from all who work for them.

The Zone 1 team climate creates a team that achieves important things with people who are excited by what they do and look forward to coming to work. The Zone 1 team climate is what we all intrinsically know as the way a workplace ought to be.

Zone 2 Team Working Climate

When the preponderance of leaders are Zone 2, their collective limitations are magnified producing some level of general inefficiency and inaction.

Zone 2 leaders and organizations primarily concentrate on limitations.

Zone 2 organizations are not operating at their potential. Interestingly, this is generally not apparent to those in charge as they tend to accept levels of performance and capacity as they are.

However, if senior leaders could see what was possible in a Zone 1 working climate, this change of perspective would make it immediately apparent that working to move all leaders into Zone 1, and thereby fostering a Zone 1 climate, is absolutely vital and should be priority #1.

In Zone 2 organizations, the collective limitations of the leaders drive the operation. The exact manifestations of this vary depending on the limitations and how they interact, especially the limitations of senior leaders, who have the most influence.

In essence, Zone 2 leaders cause many of their own problems. For instance, if the senior leaders shy away from being open, direct, or honest because they view this as confrontational, their model may become the dominant way of doing business and leaders in general may "band-aid" situations instead.

This can result in things like poor performance failing to be addressed; improper evaluation marks being assigned, and driving the morale of good performers down in reaction to this unfair and unjust treatment.

The natural human tendency is to think of self first when another person's self-centered actions affect you negatively, and Zone 2 behavior can beget Zone 2 behavior, either directly or as a second or third order effect. So when good performers have a morale drop because they have been wronged, there is no mystery why.

While Zone 2 leaders have excellent awareness, their choice in too many cases is to justify their inappropriate actions, or inaction. Again, self comfort and self-preservation come first.

Interestingly, some Zone 2 leaders will openly discuss their self-imposed disabilities. When a Zone 2 leader says things like, "I know I should talk to Sally about her performance, but she intimidates me," they are modeling what has come to be accepted in many Zone 2 climates as acceptable behaviors.

If a Zone 1 leader were to hear this, they would take action to correct this. But in a Zone 2 climate, empathy or sympathy with the plight of the Zone 2 "victim" is the more common response.

When formal mentoring systems are present in Zone 2 organizations, it is common for the senior leadership to not participate nor make having a mentor a high priority for subordinates. An additional handicap exists in Zone 2 climates in that Zone 2 leaders cannot effectively mentor others because of their limitations. In fact, it is again not uncommon to find functionally inept or failed mentoring relationships that exist for show, but which produce little value for mentees.

Zone 2 organizations foster a climate where people outwardly say they want feedback, but it is not used effectively if offered. It is not entirely uncommon for those who offer what is seen as bothersome or controversial feedback to be responded to unfavorably. It is usually made very clear that certain types of feedback are not appreciated and are discouraged. "I'm just going to keep my mouth shut," is an all too common sentiment expressed at many Zone 2 organizations.

Praise and constructive criticism are not used in a balanced manner thus creating winners and losers which results in much frustration and even personal animosity and grudges. Formal awards are bothersome to many people in Zone 2 climates and may work counter to what was intended in some cases, especially if those who are perceived as undeserving receive awards.

Accountability in Zone 2 Organizations

Zone 2 organizations tend to place uneven emphasis on appropriate responsibility and accountability. Honest and accurate grading in the evaluation system is likely to be looked at with negativity, as in how it will affect "me" if events such as layoffs occur. Grading tends to be inflated, and comments lacking in documenting actual performance. It is therefore more difficult or impossible to use evaluations to validate performance or provide accountability. Actual superior performers often feel that their evaluations are cheapened because of these inconsistencies and grade inflation.

Supervisors tend to give good marks without supporting comments in an effort to avoid accountability for themselves. Some Zone 2 leaders will also dump their responsibility on subordinates, directing them to self-evaluate and write their own evaluations.

Finally, in many Zone 2 climates, evaluations are submitted so late as to communicate to subordinates that the leadership places almost no importance on doing this for their people, and that the jobs they do have little significance.

Zone 2 climates rarely hold senior leaders properly accountable for the effectiveness of subordinate leaders under them, nor is this included in either the grading or comments in the senior leader's evaluations.

Zone 2 Team Working Climate Summary

The Zone 2 climate is marked by limitations, mostly self-imposed. Zone 2 leaders tend to be overly concerned with self in the areas that they are ineffective. This creates a fragmented workplace that usually achieves its basic purpose, but does not operate at true capacity.

Morale is haphazard and there are many opportunities for de-motivation. Zone 2 climates usually leave those who work there with the feeling of uncertainty and wanting things to change for the better.

Zone 2 climates have become quite common and have added to workers seeing their jobs as insecure environments, therefore always having their resume out there and being ready to move on if required.

Zone 3 Team Working Climate

When the preponderance of leaders are Zone 3 types, the information flow is so poor that they might blindly "walk off a cliff" together and wonder how it happened.

It is most common for the people working in a Zone 3 climate to take up the slack and make things run as they should. The interactions the team has with the Zone 3 leader are few and amount to mostly lip-service. The Zone 3 leader has no real affect on the climate, which is actually defined by those taking up the slack.

The climate created in these instances is typically Zone 2. So we end up with a Zone 2 climate being lead (on paper at least) by a Zone 3 leader who has been minimized or excluded.

A Zone 3 climate may also be formed as the result of the collective limitations of a group of Zone 2 leaders. Limitations on the effective sharing of information is the key factor that makes up this Zone 3 climate and the Zone 2 leaders involved will do this for a variety of reasons.

As an example, a "Self-disabled" Zone 2 leader may fail to share information he or she thinks is controversial or risky for fear of being held accountable. On the other hand, an "Out-for-#1" Zone 2 leader who sees information as power may fail to share the same information in an attempt to retain this perceived power. These are only two reasons that Zone 2 leaders might not share information freely; there are as many actual reasons as there are Zone 2 leader limitations.

When Zone 2 limitations collectively cause a Zone 3 climate, over-concern with self is at the heart of the problem.

Zone 2 information issues and Zone 3 "mini-climates" are often easily observable in meetings and conferences. The higher up the senior attendees or participants, the more thwarted the information flow seems to be.

Conversations in the hall during breaks or after the meeting reveal the Zone 3 nature of the group. You may hear an individual saying something like, "What a waste of time and money! The boss is way off on this thing and everyone in there knows it except her. Someone should really say something, but they're all too busy kissing up instead. I would love to, but then I'd probably be branded as insubordinate for disagreeing with them all and I'm not about to get my head chopped off."

Unfortunately this is something we've probably all experienced, and graphically illustrates the key issue in a Zone 3 climate – ineffectiveness and inefficiency caused by poor communication flow.

In some Zone 3 organizations, the leader is the sole determinant of the climate and no others have any significant input. This occurs when the Zone 3 leader shuts down all input from the team to satisfy their need to feel safe. As long as the leader is kept happy, all appears well, but this is just an illusion.

Zone 3 Team Working Climate Summary

The Zone 3 climate is marked by poor information flow. The Zone 3 leaders responsible tend to be minimized and ignored, with the rest of the team picking up the slack and making things work properly.

Key Points of Chapter Nine

1. The primary determinant of workplace climate in most cases is the Zone in which the preponderance of leaders operate.

2. The way to change the climate is to develop the leaders. They will then naturally change the climate to match their leadership zone.

3. Zone 1 leaders and organizations primarily concentrate on facts. The Zone 1 climate is what we all intrinsically know as the way a workplace ought to be.

4. Zone 2 leaders and organizations primarily concentrate on limitations, mostly self-imposed. Zone 2 climates have become quite common and have added to workers seeing their jobs as insecure environments.

5. Zone 3 leaders and organizations are marked by extremely poor communication, and the key issues in a Zone 3 working climate are ineffectiveness and inefficiency caused by this poor communication flow.

6. In some Zone 3 organizations, the leader is the sole determinant of the climate and no others have any significant input. As long as the leader is kept happy, all appears well, but this is just an illusion.

7. Most significantly, when the difference between a Zone 1 working climate and other Zone climates are examined, it becomes clear that all organizations should be working toward developing Zone 1 leaders as a primary initiative.

Chapter Ten

How to Move Your Team to Zone 1

Zone 1	Zone 2	Zone 3
- Fully Aware - Focused on others first - Fully Effective - Genuine Leader	- Fully Aware - Focused on self first - Effectiveness limited by self-centered focus - Disingenuous Leader	- Awareness and/or focus are unsteady; influenced by stress, pressure, emotions, and situations - Effectiveness is erratic - Unstable Leader

Developing a Zone 1 team working climate is a two step process. First work to develop individuals as Zone 1 leaders. Second, these Zone 1 leaders will then work to develop their team into a Zone 1 climate.

While it is the ideal that this shift to Zone 1 be a fully supported effort that starts with the top leader, there are many circumstances where this may not be the case.

The good news is that any individual leader can decide and take action to become Zone 1, and also create a Zone 1 climate with those below them.

In fact, this could be the way to move the larger climate toward Zone 1 – when others see the results; this may be the spark they need. This is true Zone 1 leadership – leading effectively from whatever position a person may hold.

Like many worthwhile initiatives, the basic steps are straightforward. We'll first look at the Zone 1 leader development process, and then discuss how to work to create a Zone 1 climate.

The Zone 1 Leader Development process

1. Understand your personality and areas of comfort.
2. Get feedback from others on your leadership performance.
3. Work with your mentor to develop goals and action plans.
4. Take action, evaluate progress and results.
5. Repeat this process for continuous improvement.

Understand your personality and areas of comfort

To know more about whom you are at your core, it is useful to get feedback from those who know you well.

Your areas of comfort usually relate to your areas of leadership effectiveness, while your areas of discomfort usually relate to your areas of leadership weakness. It is useful to spend time analyzing these areas to help identify the things you need to work on to attain Zone 1.

It is also useful to have a code, or leadership bushido, by which to measure yourself.

Get feedback from others on your leadership performance

Talk to your supervisor, peers, and trusted senior subordinates to get feedback on your leadership performance and the results it has on the team.

You are looking for specific things you are doing and if they are being interpreted as intended. You should also gain a heightened awareness of your blind areas that result in unknowingly negative results with your team.

The overall goal is finding out what others see as important for you to correct within yourself to attain Zone 1.

Work with your mentor to develop goals and action plans

Establish a mentoring relationship with a known Zone 1 leader. Define your current level of commitment to developing into a Zone 1 leader, and what your development is going to entail from this point forward.

Make your goals significant. No busy work here!

Prioritize specific weaknesses and shortfalls that you need to correct.

Set a minimum of one, but no more than three development goals. This will allow you to focus on what will have the most meaning, significance, and will produce the most substantial results. (Please see Chapter 11 for a discussion of effective development goals).

Take action, evaluate progress and results

Act with purpose and tenacity. Zone 1 development goals should be at the forefront of the way you think and act throughout your day.

Evaluate your progress continuously. Concentrate on outcomes; what are the impacts and results of your actions? Include second and third order outcomes in your awareness.

Seek accurate feedback from a balance of people. This feedback needs to come from those who will give you their honest and open critical observations. It is vital for you to understand how your natural reactions, expressions of emotion, ways of saying things, etc. affect others.

Confer with your mentor as soon as possible to discuss what you find out. Make adjustments based on your needs for growth in relation to the needs of your team and the organization as a whole. This is useful in identifying and addressing actions you find uncomfortable or difficult.

Always be open to revising your goals to ensure they remain significant. Don't be afraid to drop a goal and add a new goal.

Repeat this process for continuous improvement

Zone 1 leaders realize they will need a mentor(s) throughout their leadership life and are continuously challenging themselves for ways to enhance their performance as leaders throughout this journey.

Now let's look at how to utilize Zone 1 leadership in developing a Zone 1 Organizational Climate.

The Zone 1 Team Working Climate Development Process

1. Establish a Zone 1 leader development initiative.

2. Get feedback from all employees on team working climate.

3. Develop team goals and action plans.

4. Take action, evaluate progress and results.

5. Repeat this process for continuous improvement.

Establish a Zone 1 leader development initiative

There are three significant elements to a Zone 1 initiative:

Leadership mentoring system

> This is the key to effective Zone 1 development, therefore all leaders, including the top leader, must have a formal mentor.

> Ideally, these mentors should be Zone 1 leaders. This may not be initially possible to achieve, in which case mentors need to be as close to Zone 1 as possible, and should operate under the tutelage of a Zone 1 leader.

Accountability

> This starts with an open and honest atmosphere. Supervisors and mentors should be privy to everything pertaining to the developing leaders they are working with. This includes all feedback assessments.

> Additionally, the evaluation system, organization-wide,

must be uniform, fair, and honest. This allows it to act as an effective validation and accountability tool.

Support from the top

The top leader and all senior executive staff must be on the same page and take Zone 1 development seriously.

They must convey that this is not just another "flavor of the month" program that will come and go.

Support can only happen if there is proper involvement by the entire senior leadership team. In other words, all senior leaders must act in a Zone 1 manner immediately in order for the initiative to succeed.

Get feedback from all employees on team working climate

A team working climate survey should be conducted and repeated regularly. This allows every employee to know where things stand and work as a team to develop the climate toward Zone 1.

This survey must be designed to gather feedback about how their team is functioning and concentrate on motivation and attitude factors. It should be relatively short and stay on point.

It should not include opinion polls, questions about the physical environment, or any other items that do not directly assess how the team is functioning.

Repeating the exact same survey at regular intervals, such as annually, provides benchmarks and trend analysis which are vital facts in Zone 1 climates.

Develop team goals and action plans

In a Zone 1 climate, the results of the team working climate survey are shared with all employees, but in a very specific way. First, the executive staff reviews the climate survey and picks out any items they will take for action. They will detail their goals and plans in writing.

Individual leaders, guided by their Zone 1 mentor, will then discuss their specific team results with the entire team and work together to reach consensus and set specific goals and action plans to move the team climate toward Zone 1. They will also brief the team on items the executive staff has taken for action and review their written goals and plans. These discussions need to happen in as timely a manner as possible following completion of the survey in order to enhance their relevance.

Using the climate survey results in this way, instead of restricting who gets to see the results, will have an immediate and lasting effect on the climate. It specifically works to build esprit-de-corps, or morale, and ownership by every employee in the development of Zone 1 plans and actions. It also works to provide maximum accountability at every level resulting in the climate being the best for all employees. The time investment is minimal considering the potential outcome.

Take action, evaluate progress and results

The team and those assigned to lead specific Zone 1 team development goals should evaluate progress continuously. They should concentrate on outcomes; what are the impact and results of actions? They should seek accurate feedback from everyone affected to ensure honest and open critical observations.

The teams should discuss progress as part of their regular team meetings and make adjustments to their actions as they go to remain on track toward goal attainment. They should also be open to revising team goals and plans to ensure they remain significant.

One benefit that underlies these team efforts is that it frees the leader in terms of both time and focus because the team becomes increasingly self-directed. This allows the leader to then become more forward-looking and strategic in their focus. In fact, at some point, the leadership will likely need to strategically rethink the entire direction and way the organization does business because the evolving Zone 1 climate will result in a whole new set of organizational capacities and capabilities.

Leading a mature and focused Zone 1 team vs. a limited Zone 2 or 3 team opens up many new possibilities and opportunities, and quite frankly, is fun to lead.

Repeat this process for continuous improvement

Zone 1 organizations must be diligent at maintaining themselves in Zone 1.

Those who are part of the efforts to get to Zone 1 understand how they did it. As new people are added and older ones leave, the understanding of this experience within the team begins to fade.

New people bring their ways with them, some of which are undesirable.

If not actively maintained, even the most solidly built Zone 1 climate can erode as people adopt or revert to undesirable ways.

Zone 1 teams must challenge themselves for ways to enhance their organizations and remain in Zone 1 throughout their journey together.

The Role of Formal Assessments

A leader cannot understand the full impact of his or her actions by merely looking at the apparent outcome. We are limited in our ability to know or deduce these things by ourselves.

Leaders must know and understand the thoughts and feelings of those affected by their actions to understand the true impact.

The primary role of well designed formal assessments is to reveal this inner knowledge so that we can relate outcomes to what is intended, and track trends.

With respect to formal assessment instruments, Be a Better Boss, LLC has created and utilizes the following assessments in its consulting practice:

1. Leadership and Management Effectiveness Profile (LME);
2. Team Member Effectiveness Profile (TME);
3. Team Working Climate Survey.

And also:
4. Myers-Briggs Type Indicator® (MBTI)®

Key Points of Chapter Ten

1. Developing a Zone 1 climate is a two step process. First work to develop individuals as Zone 1 leaders. They will then work to develop those under them into the Zone 1 climate.

2. There are three significant elements to a Zone 1 initiative:
    a. Leadership mentoring System.
    b. Accountability system.
    c. Support from highest level is vital.

3. Zone 1 leaders realize they will need a mentor(s) throughout their leadership life and are continuously challenging themselves for ways to enhance themselves throughout this journey.

4. The team working climate survey should be conducted and repeated regularly in order for every employee to know where things stand and work as a team to develop the climate toward Zone 1.

5. Zone 1 organizations must be diligent at maintaining themselves in Zone 1.

Chapter Eleven
Development Goals, Plans, and Motivation

Clearly, the development of highly effective leadership skills by the person entrusted to lead a team is foundational. We owe it to those we lead to be the best leaders we can be.

When we come up against areas of personal discomfort, or identify things we know we should work on, if we retreat back to where we feel personally comfortable, we are selling ourselves, our team, the organization, and our customers short.

Every leader has something they need to improve upon. Even when you think you've reached the top of your game, something will change; staff changes, tech changes, economic changes – you name it.

The dynamics of these changes will require us to evolve our skills once again, usually in a way we couldn't have imagined... or could we?

Strategic Timeout

Many top leaders have been influenced and shaped to some extent by a man they never met named Earl Nightingale. He has been hailed as the "Dean of Personal Development" and his body of work is extensive.

One of the many impactful things he advocated we each do as leaders, is to take out a blank sheet of paper and spend some time, say 15 or 20 minutes, and brainstorm where our business will be in the future.

How will your business change in the next 5, 10, or 20 years? What will those on the forefront of development in your business field be doing by then? How and what can you change to become one of those change leaders?

It's a daunting challenge to think that way, but imagine the possibilities that taking a strategic timeout could produce. Hmm…

Consider adding this to your "To do" list and putting it on your schedule.

The Power to Change

Changing ourselves takes a measure of humility to challenge what has become the status quo in our lives as leaders. This is not an easy thing for most of us to do because it requires us to admit things we would rather not admit.

And while some of these changes will be completely within and invisible to others, they will inevitably result in some sort of change in our actions.

One element of the great internal battle that we are being asked to face, may result in our asking, "If I decide to change, just by virtue of acting differently, will I reveal my faults to others?"

In truth, to hide our faults, or cover them over from others, is all very natural. Some of us have done this so many times that it has become what we accept as "just being myself."

This implies a great truth that allows us to live with our faults; we have forgiven ourselves.

Forgiving Yourself

Forgiving ourselves is usually easy to do because we know every step we've taken, every decision we've made, and every justification we've told ourselves for why we are the way we are. This makes sense to us, and makes it easy to become blind to our own leadership shortfalls.

We can't hide who we really are in the long run. Others know, or at least suspect what our faults really are.

Again, changing ourselves will take a measure of humility to challenge what has become the status quo in our lives as leaders.

Much is being asked of you, and humility in this case means putting your false self away and becoming the best and most genuine leader you can as your primary contribution to the team you lead.

How Genuine Leaders Serve Others

To be a genuine leader means you need to serve those you lead by thinking of them first, and doing what you know to be right for them, your company, and your customers.

This is not easy, but it is right, and it is what makes a genuine leader.

You do have help in this if you seek it. Your higher-ups, your mentor, and possibly a trusted subordinate can all be there to help you. They can increase your awareness, help you keep your focus where it should be, and assist as you make little "tweaks" to fine tune your leadership and management skills.

Plus, there is still another, maybe even greater benefit to you personally for making these changes. You get to look in the mirror with renewed confidence and enjoyment at being in-charge.

The Goal Development Process

The goal development process that we'll use here may be a little different from what you've experienced in the past.

First, you should only set goals of true significance. Motivation will naturally follow:

- Revise, add, or delete your goals to keep them significant.

- Goals that lack significance tend to be easily set aside.

- If your goals don't naturally motivate you, they are probably too small or insignificant, and you should get bigger and better goals.

Second, set no more than three goals at a time:

- If these goals are of true significance, you will make large strides very quickly.

- Too many small goals tend to distract or water down action.

Most methods for goal setting concentrate on the goal statement and what should go into it. A well-stated goal is a good thing; however the time spent laying out your plans and actions is probably more important to success.

After all, it only takes a few minutes to state the goal, but may take many weeks, months, and even years to achieve it. And some goals, especially leadership development goals, may not have a firm deadline.

For example, many leaders recognize the need to develop better listening skills and habits. If you set a goal to listen better, what would the deadline be? Such "open-ended" goals are vital to achieve leadership effectiveness.

The Development Goal Model

You can use your own goal model if you choose, but please give this one consideration for what it may contain to strengthen the one you already like.

There are five specific areas in the development goal model:

1. State the goal, significance, and deadline.

2. What's been accomplished so far?

3. What still needs to be accomplished?

4. Action plan.

5. Indications of success.

Let's use a sample goal of "Overcoming Fear of Confrontation" to illustrate each of these.

State the goal, significance, and deadline

I will overcome my fear of confronting others.

I am very uncomfortable speaking to certain people on my team; they intimidate me. I feel like this is a serious limitation as a leader because I can't talk to them effectively about their job performance, especially when it's poor performance.

My initial target date to accomplish this goal is December 1st; however, it is also ongoing and will remain on my active list in perpetuity.

What's been accomplished so far?

My action up till now has been to avoid discussing things with others that might lead to confrontation, such as trying to correct a subordinate's unacceptable performance.

I've been this way for my entire life, but it has really become an issue during my last 16 years in different leadership positions.

I am also very apprehensive about giving less than perfect marks or negative comments on performance evaluations.

This has turned into a serious problem for me. I know I am not acting in the way I should as a leader, yet I feel powerless when this fear grips me.

I have come to hate this part of me as a leader and my self-esteem gets lower every time I avoid doing what I know I should be doing.

What still needs to be accomplished?

Get help and support; right now I feel all alone.

Fix this thing once and for all so I can be a good leader.

Find a way for my mentor or supervisor to hold me accountable so I can fix this thing!

Action plan

List specific daily steps I will take each day toward goal accomplishment in my schedule. (Deadline: start now, daily)

Research available books, DVD's, and possible courses of instruction that might exist to help to deal with my fears effectively (Deadline: July 28).

Stop avoiding situations that I fear might lead to confrontation. Ask my mentor and supervisor, who are both skilled at assertion, to help me develop an action plan to overcome my fears (Deadline: August 7).

Ask both my mentor and supervisor to coach me, role play with me, and help me develop a level of comfort (Deadline: Ongoing).

For accountability, review my actions and progress with my mentor during our regular weekly meeting, and with my supervisor as events occur (Deadline: Ongoing).

Indications of success

Develop confidence speaking with others about their performance and in other situations where confrontation occurs.

Have successful encounters with subordinates when talking about their performance instead of avoiding or backing down too easily. Be treated with respect by others in these situations.

Positive feedback from my mentor and supervisor based on actual successful encounters.

Positive feedback from my team on our next annual team working climate survey.

Your Development Goals

Set goals for yourself

Set at least one, but no more than three development goals and action plans of true significance for yourself as a leader.

Use areas of discomfort and things you know you need to work on:

1. The 3 most important things you need to change (pg 17).

2. Your leadership bushido (pg-24).

3. Your leadership & management self-evaluation (pg-41).

4. Things to ponder and fine points (pgs 43-81).

5. Insights on leadership Zones.

Set goals with your team

Again, generate at least one, but no more than three development goals and action plans, of true significance, with your team.

They key difference is "with your team." You should get together with them and determine the most significant things to work on as a team.

It would be best if the inputs came from either the team itself, or from a recent team climate survey. You should lead and facilitate the discussion rather than tell the team what you'd like to do.

This builds automatic buy-in and sets the proper tone and precedence.

Caution: Once you start this process with your team, you must carry it through to completion of goal achievement, or risk all the negatives for the team that go along with that.

You can use appropriate things you noted from those same areas of discomfort and things you know you need to work on as a team:

1. Your leadership bushido (pg-24).

2. Your leadership & management self-evaluation (pg-41).

3. Any of the points to ponder and fine points (pgs 43-81).

4. Insights on leadership Zones and team working climate.

Your Motivation

At first glance, making changes appears simple:

1. Set a goal.
2. Make a plan.
3. Follow the plan.

1, 2, 3 – easy; except for step 3.

We all know that step 3 is where we fail, and eventually drop our goals. Steps 1 and 2 may take a few minutes; step 3 might take the rest of your life.

Step 3 is why only goals of true significance can motivate us long enough to have the tenacity it takes.

In the long run, step 3 is virtually the only reason we fail!

By effectively carrying out step 3, we can defeat hopelessness and cynical attitudes. Defeating step 3 makes change possible, even if we've failed many times in the past.

Defeating step 3 (follow the plan) by setting goals of significance, is the key difference between getting motivated and staying motivated.

Other motivation factors

When I was a poor leader, I used to count a day as being a "good day," when nothing bad happened.

And if something bad did happen, the scale shifted; it was still okay if the day didn't totally suck. My standards were that low.

Setting goals of significance was easy – I had no shortage of significant goals.

What kept me from being motivated were depression and a feeling of isolation. I felt all alone in my suffering.

There are many other reasons I, or you, might not be motivated. That's why we need great mentors in our lives.

Let's investigate that in the next chapter; mentors and mentees.

Key Points of Chapter Eleven

1. Development goals are essential to dealing with issues and becoming a genuine leader in Zone 1.

2. We should only set goals of true significance because motivation will naturally follow them.

3. Set no more than three goals at a time.

4. There are five specific areas in the development goal model:

   a. State the goal, significance, and deadline.

   b. What's been accomplished so far?

   c. What still needs to be accomplished?

   d. Action plan.

   e. Indications of Success.

5. In the long run, step 3 (follow the plan) is virtually the only reason we fail!

6. Defeating step 3 (follow the plan) by setting goals of significance, is the key difference between getting motivated and staying motivated.

7. Once you start the process of generating and achieving development goals with your team, you must carry it through to completion of goal achievement, or risk all the negatives for the team that go along with that.

Chapter Twelve

Mentors and Mentees

Without good mentors, most of us would not be as good at leading others as we are. Some of us might not be leaders at all.

Left on our own, we are likely to founder; it's simply harder to go it alone.

There is great strength in being able to bounce things off a trusted friend and advisor whose primary purpose in life is to help you.

Every leader, no matter how senior or how good a leader, needs a mentor. In fact, one true test of leadership maturity is in knowing that you need a mentor and always will.

Actually, you may need several mentors depending on the needed expertise, experience, or type of person you need to relate to.

Your mentor is also there to hold you accountable, especially during those times when you just want to do the easy thing; retreat to your comfort zone, or give up.

Choosing your mentors

The number one requirement for being an effective mentor is to be a Zone 1 leader. Your mentor need not be perfect, but they need the depth of awareness and focus that Zone 1 leaders bring to the table.

Here are some other characteristics and factors you should consider:

Effective mentors should:

1. Want to be your mentor.

2. Have time, energy, and ability to meet face-to-face.

3. Be someone you can relate to easily.

4. Have a positive attitude.

5. Be a good listener and communicator.

6. Be a good advisor, an effective coach.

7. Be an open and honest communicator.

8. Be willing to offer honest feedback.

9. Be willing to serve as a sounding board.

10. Help you set clear goals and plans.

11. Be willing to hold you accountable.

12. Share from their experience, but know their limitations; admit it when another person should be consulted or called in to assist.

Effective mentors should not:

1. Make decisions for the mentee or do the work for the mentee.

2. Be anything but a trusted friend; a coach; a counselor; a fellow seeker of wisdom; and a motivator.

Developing the relationship

Effective mentoring relationships can take a long time to develop, or just click right into place with ease. There is no way to tell.

Conversely, if the relationship isn't working and a different mentor would be better for you, then it must be viewed as a "No harm, no foul" situation. This is one thing to be sure that you and your mentor discuss in the first meeting, before any commitments are made.

Here are some guidelines of what you need to discuss with your mentor early on to get the relationship off on the right foot:

1. Learn about each other and build a personal relationship:

   a. Talk about topics not pertaining to work: news and events, family history, hobbies, movies, sports, likes and dislikes, politics, etc.

   b. Share career stories including your work history, high and low points, others you've worked with and for, work experiences.

   c. Discuss both of your personal values and how these affect you at work, especially in relations with others.

2. Discuss the mentoring relationship and come to agreement on how you will work together:

   a. Negotiate ground rules, when and how you will meet; confidentiality, etc.

   b. Discuss both the mentee and mentor vision and expectations for the mentoring relationship.

   c. Discuss what each of you sees as the boundaries of the mentoring relationship.

   d. Discuss your mentee and mentor responsibilities.

   e. Discuss how feedback will be given and received, and what, if anything, either would like to avoid doing.

   f. Discuss meeting times and schedule on your calendars.

   g. Discuss how you will communicate between meetings.

3. Discuss meeting agendas and discussion framework:

   a. Will you agree on an agenda before each meeting?

   b. Are there any items you will discuss at every meeting such as mentee development goal progress?

   c. Is there a set structure / time allotment(s) you want to follow?

4. Discuss how you will deal with disagreement or even conflict with each other should they occur.

5. Discuss that a "No harm, no foul" policy should exist between you if either of you thinks that it would be a good idea for you to change mentors.

When you meet, you should

1. Meet face-to-face whenever possible.

2. Follow the meeting agenda (if agreed upon).

3. You should take the initiative to:

   a. Bring forth items for discussion in an open and honest manner. Mentor / mentee relationships are enhanced when the mentee proactively takes responsibility for what will be discussed.

   b. Initiate discussions of work events and occurrences.

   c. Ensure all discussions end with clarity, especially about who is responsible to do what, specifics, etc. Remember, the mentee has primary responsibility for determining and carrying out actions.

4. Offer and receive feedback in a useful manner. Good feedback is constructive in nature, respectful in intent, honest but not hurtful, thoughtful and thought provoking. Receive feedback with thankfulness, and try not to be overly self-critical, which is taking it personally. Look forward toward constructive changes.

5. Discuss your development goal progress and revise as necessary:

   a. In addition to accomplishments, be sure to discuss pitfalls and issues such as resistance, motivation, procrastination, scheduling issues, lessons learned, etc.

   b. Remember, goals must remain significant. They should be revised or replaced as necessary.

6. Discuss difficulties or stresses you are facing (deadlines,

conflicts, fears, inter-personal and at work relationship issues, motivation, self-esteem, etc.). Plan ways to deal with these effectively.

7. Discuss communication issues (speaking, interpreting, listening, etc.) that have experienced or successfully avoided.

8. Talk about team interactions, relationships, issues, fairness, communication, sharing work, sharing duties and responsibilities, etc.

9. Discuss how the mentor / mentee relationship is working between the two of you. Pay particular attention to honesty, trust, openness, respectfulness, and effectiveness at helping the mentee in the way(s) he or she needs.

10. Other items you want to bring to the table should be discussed.

Key Points of Chapter Twelve

1. Every leader, no matter how senior or how good a leader they may be, needs a mentor.

2. You may need several mentors depending what type of expertise, experience, or type of person you need to relate to.

3. The number one requirement for being an effective mentor is to be a Zone 1 leader.

4. A "No harm, no foul" policy should exist between you if either one of you thinks that it would be a good idea for you to change mentors.

5. Meet face-to-face whenever possible.

Appendix

A Collection of Key Points

Zone 1	Zone 2	Zone 3
- Fully Aware - Focused on others first - Fully Effective - Genuine Leader	- Fully Aware - Focused on self first - Effectiveness limited by self-centered focus - Disingenuous Leader	- Awareness and/or focus are unsteady; influenced by stress, pressure, emotions, and situations - Effectiveness is erratic - Unstable Leader

Chapter One: Three Bricks in Your Foundation

1. Leadership is influence.

2. To be influential leaders, we must have accurate awareness.

3. A leader's focus should be outward; toward their team. They should do what is right for their team above themselves.

4. Genuine leaders operate outside their comfort zones, being faithful to the team and putting them first.

5. Never give up. Instead find a good mentor and work to fix what you need to fix.

6. A true friend and mentor will help you stand up, fight, and change.

Chapter Two: Leadership Bushido

1. If you have no idea who you are or what you are all about, then your team won't be able to count on you, and will have no confidence in you.

2. A code is not a set of rules; it's a set of guiding principles.

3. Twenty-one is a nice number!

Chapter Five: Leadership Zones

1. Leadership skills are a unique skill-set, different from other skills such as technical or professional skills.

2. Leaders may settle into zones of comfort, or zones that avoid discomfort. While either of these may seem personally correct, they can be destructive if they are not also right for the team.

3. Leadership is about influencing people, while management is about organization; process and procedure.

4. Zone 1 leaders are fully effective genuine leaders.

5. Zone 1 leadership skills can be developed as we

acknowledge our limitations and use them to our advantage.

Chapter Six: Zone 1 Leaders

1. Both natural and developed leaders operate in Zone 1 as fully effective genuine leaders.

2. Zone 1 leaders make fewer and fewer mistakes as they continually develop. They strive to make each mistake only once, correct it, and then grow from it.

3. Zone 1 leaders have the ability to read and react to what is right for the team as things develop. They are not stuck in any pre-conceived box.

4. In order to be a fully effective Zone 1 leader, you must also be a fully effective manager.

5. Selfless service is one hallmark of being a genuine leader.

Chapter Seven: Zone 2 Leaders

1. Zone 2 leaders are fully aware of their weaknesses.

2. Every time you see a failing leader that is not being helped effectively, you are actually seeing at least two failing leaders, because it is the higher-up leader's responsibility to make sure their subordinate leaders are effective.

3. Zone 2 leaders may want to see themselves as being Zone 1 except for having some shortfalls. But this is not valid in reality because part time effectiveness is simply not the

same as being a genuine leader.

4. Zone 1 leaders are genuine leaders and do not shift back and forth from other zones.

Chapter Eight: Zone 3 Leaders

1. Care needs to be taken when choosing who to put in charge, whether in an interim situation or as part of the regular selection process. Zone 3 leaders are usually a poor choice and the team will usually suffer for it.

2. Zone 3 leaders can develop themselves into Zone 1, with proper assistance and mentoring from a Zone 1 leader.

3. Zone 3 leaders are frequently in a very scary place, and so may be very open to changing.

Chapter Nine: Team Working Climate

1. The primary determinant of workplace climate in most cases is the Zone in which the preponderance of leaders operates.

2. The way to change the climate is to develop the leaders. They will then naturally change the climate to match their leadership zone.

3. Zone 1 leaders and organizations primarily concentrate on facts. The Zone 1 climate is what we all intrinsically know as the way a workplace ought to be.

4. Zone 2 leaders and organizations primarily concentrate on

limitations, mostly self-imposed. Zone 2 climates have become quite common and have added to workers seeing their jobs as insecure environments.

5. Zone 3 leaders and organizations are marked by extremely poor communication, and the key issues in a Zone 3 working climate are ineffectiveness and inefficiency caused by this poor communication flow.

6. In some Zone 3 organizations, the leader is the sole determinant of the climate and no others have any significant input. As long as the leader is kept happy, all appears well, but this is just an illusion.

7. Most significantly, when the difference between a Zone 1 working climate and other Zone climates are examined, it becomes clear that all organizations should be working toward developing Zone 1 leaders as a primary initiative.

Chapter Ten: How to Move Your Team to Zone 1

1. Developing a Zone 1 climate is a two step process. First work to develop individuals as Zone 1 leaders. They will then work to develop those under them into the Zone 1 climate.

2. There are three significant elements to a Zone 1 initiative:
   a. Leadership mentoring system
   b. Accountability
   c. Support from the top

3. Zone 1 Leaders realize they will need a mentor(s) throughout their leadership life and are continuously challenging themselves for ways to enhance themselves

throughout this journey.

4. The team working climate survey should be conducted and repeated regularly in order for every employee to know where things stand and work as a team to develop the climate toward Zone 1.

5. Zone 1 organizations must be diligent at maintaining themselves in Zone 1.

Chapter Eleven: Development Goals, Plans, and Motivation

1. Development goals are essential to dealing with issues and becoming a genuine leader in Zone 1.

2. We should only set goals of true significance because motivation will naturally follow them.

3. Set no more than three goals at a time.

4. There are five specific areas in the development goal model:

    a. State the goal, significance, and deadline.

    b. What's been accomplished so far?

    c. What still needs to be accomplished?

    d. Action plan.

    e. Indications of Success.

5. In the long run, step 3 (follow the plan) is virtually the only reason we fail!

6. Defeating step 3 (follow the plan) by setting goals of significance, is the key difference between getting motivated and staying motivated.

7. Once you start the process of generating and achieving development goals with your team, you must carry it through to completion of goal achievement, or risk all the negatives for the team that go along with that.

Chapter Twelve: Mentors and Mentees

1. Every leader, no matter how senior or how good a leader they may be, needs a mentor.

2. You may need several mentors depending what type of expertise, experience, or type of person you need to relate to.

3. The number one requirement for being an effective mentor is to be a Zone 1 leader.

4. A "No harm, no foul" policy should exist between you if either one of you thinks that it would be a good idea for you to change mentors.

5. Meet face-to-face whenever possible.

A Final Word From the Author

Have a cup of coffee with me and let me share a thought or two.

Leadership goes far beyond getting the team to produce.

Your leadership is reflected in the lives of those you lead, and being a good leader takes conscious effort, creativity, tenacity, and just a bit of respectful humility too.

Remember to be aware of the impact of your actions – how others think and feel – and when it goes wrong for you, stand up and take responsibility to make changes.

That's what leaders do.

I hope that this book was eye opening, impactful, and helpful as you take on the challenge of working to turn your limitations into strengths.

I encourage you to always be open, always be learning, and wish you happiness and success in your life as a leader and manager.

Aloha!
Robert S. Walsh

To help you develop yourself and your team further, the tools on the following pages are available at www.BeaBetterBoss.com

Your team deserves you to be the best leader possible.

Likewise, you deserve the personal reward of self-confidence that comes from being the most effective leader you can be.

The Leadership & Management Effectiveness (LME) Profile gives you insights from the most reliable sources ever created - those who know you.

Learn how they see you in these ten areas of leadership competency:

Communication - Feedback - Emotions - Teamwork
Delegation - Judgment and Decision Making
Self-Management - Organization and Planning
Leadership & Influence - Honesty and Integrity

Then let the LME take you through acting on this knowledge to make meaningful changes.

Like the best leaders you know - when they find something that needs fixing, they fix it - and that's what makes them the best.

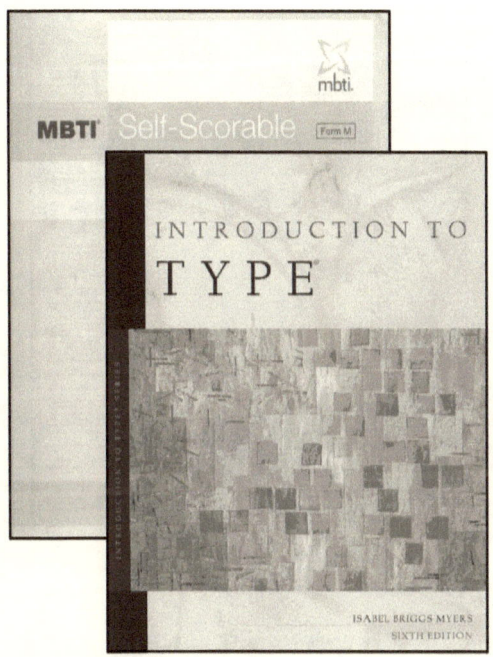

MBTI ® Workshop for Groups and Teams

The MBTI ®Team workshop is four hours (4 hrs) long and includes:

The hard-copy MBTI® Form M Instrument for each participant;

1. A copy of the "Introduction to Type" workbook for each participant;

2. Facilitated group discussion of MBTI® by a Certified MBTI® practitioner;

3. Interactive group discussions and exercises for participants to gain understanding of how to apply type preference knowledge to improve team efficiency, effectiveness, and team working climate.

4. Works great as a "10 to 2" session with working lunch!

We'd love to help you build your leadership team!

Everyone wants to work for a strong leader on a great team.

You can build your team stronger by tapping the knowledge of your people in these six key areas:

Self-determination
Engagement
Standards
Feedback
Comprehensibility
Esprit de Corps

Many important changes are possible; changes that are right on target because they started with insights from your team.

Plus we'll help you transform those insights into action with our Team Improvement Process Guide; included your survey report.

You know, there's just nothing better than looking forward to coming to work each day because the team you're on is solid.

Act now – get a price quote. We'll also send you a sample survey report and an action proposal. Your team is worth it.

Training and Development Services
from Be a Better Boss, LLC

"The greatest discovery of my generation is that human beings can alter their lives by altering their attitude of mind." - William James

What we believe...

Purposeful leadership development efforts require facilitation by a person who can artfully "step on toes" in just the right way. They need to be able to influence participants to "alter their attitude of mind" by getting them to:

- do an honest self-reflection;
- clearly define what they need to do;
- understand why they need to do it;
- have the courage to start;
- have the motivation to tenaciously see it through.

Leadership trainers and coaches also need to be involved with mentors and supervisors. Program participants need this level of support and accountability as they implement changes, but this level of involvement is unfortunately rare.

While well designed curriculum and course materials are important management functions, many people can do them effectively.

Success depends on having a genuine leader conduct the program; one who can not only teach and coach, but who embodies the characteristics of proper leadership.

Your people need a good example right there in front of them, because people do what they see.

These are the things we believe. Your team knows what makes a good initiative worthwhile, and we ask that you consider us to provide that for you.

Your team deserves your best efforts, and likewise, you deserve to work with great teammates.

You deserve the personal reward of self-confidence that comes from being the most effective professionally at what you do.

The Team Member Effectiveness (TME) Profile gives you insights from the most reliable sources ever created - those who know you.

Learn how they see you in these ten areas of leadership competency:

Communication - Feedback - Emotions - Teamwork
Responsibility - Judgment and Decision Making
Self-Management - Knowledge and Professional Performance
Motivation - Honesty and Integrity

Then let the TME take you through acting on this knowledge to make meaningful changes.

Like the best colleagues you work with - when they find something that needs fixing, they fix it - and that's what makes them the best.

www.BeaBetterBoss.com